Calico Jack, Anne Bonny and Mary Read: The Lives and Legacies of History's Most Famous Pirate Crew

By Charles River Editors

Calico Jack's "Jolly Roger" pirate flag

About Charles River Editors

Charles River Editors was founded by Harvard and MIT alumni to provide superior editing and original writing services, with the expertise to create digital content for publishers across a vast range of subject matter. In addition to providing original digital content for third party publishers, Charles River Editors republishes civilization's greatest literary works, bringing them to a new generation via ebooks.

Introduction

Calico Jack Rackham (1682-1720)

"The Day that Rackam was executed, by special Favour, he was admitted to see [Anne Bonny]; but all the Comfort she gave him, was, that she was sorry to see him there, but if he had fought like a Man, he need not have been hang'd like a Dog." - Captain Charles Johnson, *A General History of the Robberies and Murders of the most notorious Pyrates*

One of the most famous pirates of all time is Calico Jack, and though he would accomplish many things in his career that would earn him notoriety among the pirates of his age, the simple truth is that he is remembered mostly for his association with Anne Bonny and Mary Read, two of history's most famous women pirates. In fact, had it not been for his involvement with them, his name might have disappeared from the history books entirely. And fittingly, even his nickname, "Calico," came from the type of fabric he preferred for his shirts, the same fabric typically used for women's everyday clothing. Rackham preferred attractive print fabrics produced for trade with natives in the New World, a flamboyant taste worthy of the common pirate stereotype.

Before Rackham had even met Anne Bonny, who would become his lover, he had managed to make a name for himself as part of Charles Vane's pirate crew, and it was after a mutiny that he became the captain of a pirate ship. This would allow Calico Jack to make yet another contribution to pirate history and legend: the "Jolly Roger" pirate flag. Flying the simple yet frightening flag that featured a white skull and crossed swords against a black banner, Calico Jack ensured his targets knew they were in trouble as soon as they could spot the flag. To this day, the flag remains synonymous with piracy.

Still, it seems Calico Jack will never escape the shadow of his famous female shipmates, despite the fact he was their captain. For his part, Jack never seems to have minded the women who stood beside and behind him through most of his short career, and if anything it seems he enjoyed having the fairer sex aboard, in more ways than one. Their most adventurous and notorious year, 1720, would also be Rackham's last, after they were eventually caught by authorities and tried. In one of the Golden Age of Piracy's most famous anecdotes, one of Calico Jack's last wishes was to see Anne Bonny one more time, and she "consoled" him by telling him that if he fought like a man he wouldn't have been hanged like a dog.

Calico Jack, Anne Bonny and Mary Read looks at the mysterious life and legends of the famous pirate, attempting to separate fact from fiction while analyzing his lasting legacy. Along with pictures depicting Calico Jack and important people, places, and events in his life, you will learn about the pirate captain like you never have before, in no time at all.

18th century depiction of Anne Bonny and Mary Read

Anne Bonny (1702-??) and Mary Read (??-1721)

"NOW we are to begin a History full of surprizing Turns and Adventures; I mean, that of Mary Read and Anne Bonny, alias Bonn, which were the true Names of these two Pyrates; the odd Incidents of their rambling Lives are such, that some may be tempted to think the whole Story no better than a Novel or Romance; but since it is supported by many thousand Witnesses, I mean the People of Jamaica, who were present at their Tryals, and heard the Story of their Lives, upon the first discovery of their Sex; the Truth of it can be no more contested, than that there were such Men in the World, as Roberts and Black-beard..." - Captain Charles Johnson, *A General History of the Robberies and Murders of the most notorious Pyrates*

One of the most famous pirates of all time, and possibly the most famous woman to ever become one, was Anne Bonny. The Irish-born girl moved with her family to the Bahamas at a young age in the early 18th century, which at that time was a hotbed for piracy by the likes of Blackbeard, but the redhead with a fiery temper would go on to forge her own reputation. After marrying a poor sailor who accepted clemency to give up piracy, Anne began a legendary affair with Calico Jack Rackam and became pregnant with his child, but that did not stop them from plundering the high seas aboard his pirate ship *Revenge*, at least until they were captured by British authorities. Anne avoided execution by "pleading her belly", getting a temporary stay of execution due to her pregnancy.

It is at that point that Anne Bonny drops off the historical record and becomes the stuff of legends. It's unclear whether she was eventually executed or pardoned or even ransomed, and it's unclear what became of her child. Her relationship with Mary Read aboard the Revenge is also the stuff of legends, and people have been filling in the gaps ever since.

Among all the pirates of the "Golden Age of Piracy", none were as unique as Mary Read, who was one of just two known women to be tried as a pirate during the Golden Age, alongside her own crewmate (and possible lover) Anne Bonny. Like Anne, Mary Read was an illegitimate child who spent some of her childhood dressed up as and disguised as a little boy through incredibly strange circumstances. But unlike her future shipmate, Mary ultimately took a liking to it, and she continued to disguise her gender to take on roles reserved for men, including in the British army. During that time, she fell in love with a Flemish soldier and eventually married him.

Mary Read might have been content to live out her life with her husband in Holland, but after his death, she headed for the West Indies, only to have her ship commandeered by pirates. But Read, who had worked on a ship before, was only too happy to join the pirate crew and play the role of privateer. And in 1720, that crew was captured by Calico Jack, who already had his lover Anne Bonny as part of his crew and now unwittingly added a second female when Mary opted to join.

Together the three played a legendary role as shipmates and possible lovers while continuing their piracy around the Bahamas, only to eventually be captured by authorities in October 1720. Most of the crew was executed, but Mary was able to successfully "plead the belly" and thereby receiving a stay of execution. This spared her the noose, but Mary would die of illness while still imprisoned in 1721.

Calico Jack, Anne Bonny and Mary Read looks at the mysterious lives and legends of the two famous female pirates, attempting to separate fact from fiction while analyzing their lasting legacies. Along with pictures depicting Anne Bonny, Mary Read, and other important people, you will learn about the famous pirates like you never have before.

Chapter 1: Mary Read's Early Years

According to legend, Mary Read was born sometime between 1670-1698 in London, England. The sole contemporary account of her life, written anonymously by someone using the pseudonym Captain Charles Johnson, references Mary's husband as having died sometime around the Peace of Ryswick, which ended the Nine Years War in 1697. If that was correct, Mary had to have been born in the 1670s. Some modern historians believe it's more likely Mary's husband died sometime after the Treaty of Utrecht, which ended the War of the Spanish Succession in 1713. That makes Mary's date of birth more likely to be sometime around 1690.

Whatever the case, even from her earliest days of existence, Mary's life was shaped by the sea and the men who sailed on it. Her mother appears to have married a sailor while she was still rather young and became pregnant, but after he returned to the sea word eventually came back to her that he had met with an accident and died. Before she had time to fully cope, she had given birth to her first child, a son.

With her husband dead, the young Mrs. Read was forced to depend on her wealthy mother-in-law for support. However, this plan quickly fell through when she met another young man, probably a sailor, and found herself pregnant again. She knew that if the older woman found out what had happened, she would be left with no support at all and probably lose custody of her son in the process. Thus, she left town for a place where she could continue to pass herself off as a tragic young widow. She may have planned to put her new baby up for adoption and then return to her mother-in-law as if nothing had happened, or she may have hoped that, with her new reputation as the tragic widowed mother, she could find a new husband.

However, once Mrs. Read reached her new town tragedy struck once again, this time taking the life of her infant son. It was around this time that Mrs. Read came up with a cunning plan; if her new child was a boy, she could remain away long enough to let him "catch up" with the older baby's age and them pass him off as her first child, once more returning to her mother-in-law's good graces.

Unfortunately for Mrs. Read, fate had other plans, and she soon gave birth to a healthy baby girl named Mary. She may not have had the boy she desired, but the determined young woman saw no reason for the child's gender to thwart her plans, and she began to immediately dress young Mary in her dead brother's clothes. This was made easier by the fact that boys and girls in 17th century Europe both wore dresses until they were five or six years old. Her plan succeeded, and the elder Mrs. Read became once more enamored of her little grandson and continued to support them until her death.

As Mary's mother continued the ruse, little Mary found that she not only enjoyed dressing like a boy but also loved having access to the freedom that the life of a boy afforded her. Though her mother explained to her when she was old enough to understand that she was not actually a boy like other boys, Mary chose to continue to live as if she had been born male. After her grandmother died, her mother was again destitute and again hatched a plan to use her daughter to support her. Mary was by this time 13 years old, and when dressed in male clothing she looked very much the part of the effeminate footmen that the French nobility of that time preferred.

Before long, however, Mary grew tired of the restrictions of her life in the home of a nobleman and decided to seek her fortune elsewhere. She began by joining the crew of a British Man of War, but at first she found that life at sea was not to her particular liking. It may have been that she found it difficult to conceal her true gender within the cramped quarters of a sailing ship, but at the same time she was still just a teenager. She may very well have been intimidated by the rough and tumble life of a British sailor.

Whatever her reasons, she soon left the navy and joined the British army as a foot soldier. Though she did well in battle and was brave under fire, she soon realized that her family background was not sufficiently noble to earn her a commission as an officer in the infantry. As a result, she transferred again, this time to the cavalry, where she earned high praise for her ability to ride and shoot. It is unclear where she might have learned these skills, but the most likely place was while she was employed by the French nobleman.

It was while in the cavalry that Mary's life as a man came to an abrupt end. While she was in Holland she found herself fighting alongside a Flemish soldier and often spending evenings talking to him by the fireside. Before long, she found that she was no longer taking care of either her gear or herself, with her mind constantly wandering back to her Flemish comrade. She also found herself volunteering for increasingly dangerous missions, if for no reason than to fight by his side and help protect him. As Johnson quipped in *A General History of the Pyrates*, "Mars and Venus could not be served at the same Time."

As their feelings for each other intensified, the men with whom she served began to be suspicious, as did the object of her affection. When rumors began to fly about the camp that she might be homosexual, she decided to "come out of the closet" in a most unusual way: she admitted to her Flemish love that she was, in fact, a woman. The soldier, perhaps relieved that he had not fallen in love with another man, was thrilled to discover that she was in fact female, because it seemed to afford him the chance to take up his own personal mistress in camp. Johnson explained, "He was much surprized at what he found out, and not a little pleased, taking it for granted, that he should have a Mistress solely to himself, which is an unusual Thing in a Camp, since there is scarce one of those Campaign Ladies, that is ever true to a Troop or Company…"

While his initial intentions appear to have been strictly to make her his mistress, he soon discovered that she was not that willing to enter into a sexual relationship without the security of marriage. It's possible that Mary understood the price her mother paid for bearing her as an illegitimate daughter and was determined to avoid that fate herself.

For his part, her Flemish comrade eventually grew tired of waiting and proposed that they marry as soon as they could. Thus, when the army went into its summer quarters, they pooled their wages and bought her some simple, female clothing. Thus dressed, she broke the news to the company commander, who responded better than they had hoped and allowed her to leave the army with no blot on her record. Upon that, they were able to marry, and needless to say, the wedding between two former soldiers attracted much attention in the camp and led to the soldiers putting together, from their limited salaries, a sizable amount of cash for the newlyweds to begin their life together.

Using the money that they were given, as well as a little they had saved from their mutual salaries, the young couple bought an inn named The Three Horseshoes near Breda in Holland. Mary traded her breeches for petticoats and her gun for mugs of ale. There they did a good business, attracting many of their former brothers-in-arms, as well as others who heard their story and wanted to see the famous couple for themselves. But tragedy seemed to have an affinity for the Read family, and Mary's comfortably happy life ended when her husband died and left her a widow. Unable to continue to run the busy inn on her own, Mary returned to the only work she knew: soldiering. She cut her hair short again, pulled her sailor trousers out of the trunk and returned to Holland and the life of a foot soldier.

Mary obviously couldn't return to her cavalry division now that they knew her true gender, so instead she volunteered for out-of-the-way outposts with very few men, banking on the odds that she would not run into anyone who would recognize her. But this time, her plan to go to war was thwarted by peace. She soon realized that there was little hope of advancement within the confines of the peacetime military. Thus, instead of remaining in the army and waiting for her luck to run out, she boarded a merchant ship bound for the West Indies. In a new land, she might have reasoned, she would have new opportunities.

Chapter 2: Anne Cormac

18th century depiction of Anne Bonny

"Anne was not one of his legitimate Issue, which seems to cross an old Proverb, which says, that *Bastards have the best Luck.*" – Captain Charles Johnston, *A General History of the Pyrates*

The story of Anne Bonny, and perhaps her ultimate fate, was set before she was even born. Her father, William Cormac, was a prominent Irish lawyer in County Cork who had been married a year or two when his wife gave birth to their first child. The birth was somewhat traumatic and it was decided that she would go to his mother's home to rest and recover. To keep the house running while his wife was gone, Cormac hired a young woman named Peg Brennan. During the wife's absence, Cormac and Brennan became romantically entangled, and not long after his wife returned, she discovered their misadventures and began to plan her revenge.

Her first step was to return to the home of the elder Mrs. Cormac and share with her what her son had been up to. Wife and mother then joined forces to see to it that Cormac lived to regret his actions. He was cut off from all his family's money and told that his wife would never return to him. The wife also accused Brennan of stealing some family silver and had her thrown in jail, where she remained for about six months. During this time the wife's anger against her waned, and after learning that the girl was pregnant, she dropped the charges against her. Brennan was released and returned to her own home, where she delivered a healthy baby girl, Anne, on March 8, 1702.

Not long after Anne was born, the younger Mrs. Cormac gave birth herself to twins, a boy and a girl. They appear to have been conceived during the short time between her return to Cork and her discovery of her husband's infidelity. By this time the, elder Mrs. Cormac was dying and called for her son to be reconciled to his wife for the sake of the two babies, but he refused and questioned if the children were even his, since they were born so soon after his wife's journey away from him.

Angered by her son's refusal to restore his family, the elder Mrs. Cormac changed her will, leaving all her money in trust for the care of her legitimate grandchildren and the younger Mrs. Cormac. She then died, still estranged from her son. Following her death, Cormac fell on hard times, so his wife, still feeling some affection, began to provide for him out of her inheritance.

Nevertheless, during this time Cormac had also kept up his relationship with Peg Brennan, though at something of a distance. They wrote to each other regularly, and he was kept well informed of the growth and development of young Anne. When the little girl was about five years old, he decided that he would like the chance to get to know her better, so he invited her to come and live with him. However, he knew that if his wife found out, she would not be pleased and might very well cut off his allowance.

To get around this potential problem, he hatched a cunning plan. He wrote to Brennan and told her to cut the child's hair and dress her as a boy. She could then send her to him by carriage but not come herself, and he would subsequently tell the community that Anne was actually the son of a distant relative who had been sent to apprentice as a law clerk. The plan worked for a while, and father and daughter finally got to know one another, but Mrs. Cormac eventually discovered that the boy was actually Brennan's daughter. This proved to be more than Mrs. Cormac could stand, and she immediately cut off her husband's allowance.

For his part, William realized that without the money he had nothing to lose, so instead of sending Anne back to live with her mother, he brought Peg to live with them. While this had the desired effect of upsetting and embarrassing his wife, it also brought him into public disrepute in the community and resulted in a serious decline in his law practice. When he was no longer able to support himself and figured that his life in Ireland was ruined, William decided to cut his losses and try his hand in the New World. He sold everything he had except the clothes on his back and, taking Peg and Anne with him, boarded a sailing ship bound for the Carolinas, ultimately settling in the Bahamas.

William quickly tried to establish a new law practice, but he discovered in short order that there was less demand for lawyers there in the early 18th century. Eventually William turned to merchandising, which suited him better, and for the next several years he and Peg lived together as man and wife while he bought and sold goods in the coastal town where they had landed. Before long, he had amassed a sufficient fortune that allowed him to purchase a rice plantation, where he and his family lived happily for a few more years until Peg's death. By this time, Anne was about 13 and considered a young woman more than capable of taking over her mother's duties as mistress of the plantation.

Chapter 3: Anne Bonny

"She was of a fierce and couragious Temper, wherefore, when she lay under Condemnation, several Stories were reported of her, much to her Disadvantage, as that she had kill'd an English Servant-Maid once in her Passion with a Case-Knife, while she look'd after her Father's House; but upon further Enquiry, I found this Story to be groundless: It was certain she was so robust, that once, when a young Fellow would have lain with her, against her Will, she beat him so, that he lay ill of it a considerable Time." – Captain Charles Johnson, *A General History of the Pyrates*

At 13, the slender and athletic Anne was considered very good looking. She had her parents' Irish coloring, with creamy skin, flaming red hair and pea green eyes. She also had a remarkable amount of grace and balance for a girl of her time, probably due in part to the fact she spent some of her early life romping and playing outdoors as a "boy" instead of sitting and sewing by the fire. But Anne also had a fiery temper to match her red hair, and she was known throughout the community for giving anyone that crossed her a piece of her mind. Sometimes, if they were not careful, they might get something else; on at least one occasion, she attacked a servant girl with a case knife, and the anonymous author who wrote *A General History of the Pyrates* under the pseudonym Captain Charles Johnson suggested that she actually killed the girl. And while Anne no longer dressed as a boy, it seems she still fought like one. On another occasion, when she was alone in the house or out for a walk, a young man attacked her with the intention of raping her. However, he soon regretted his attempt when she fought back so fiercely that she beat him unconscious. Though he survived the attack, he was apparently out of commission for some time and never tried anything like that with her again.

One might think that such a dangerous young woman would have a problem finding a husband, but in the early 18th century there were very few available women living in the Bahamas. As a result, those who were there had no problem finding young, single men to court them. Also, by this time, Anne was the only daughter of a wealthy plantation owner, making her all the more attractive as a match. Unfortunately for her father and potential suitors, Anne's temper and rebellious streak made her turn up her nose at all the nicer young men from good families that her father brought home to meet her. Fittingly, Anne was attracted to the shadier rogues instead, and when she was 16 years old, she fell in love with James Bonny, a poor sailor with rumored underworld connections.

When she told her father of her new beau, he flew into a rage and informed her that the word around the island was that Bonny was a pirate, and that he was probably only interested in her for her money. He forbade Anne to see him again and threatened to disinherit her if she did not end the relationship immediately. Of course, such threats meant nothing to the hard-headed girl, and her father's disapproval may well have made Bonny even more attractive to her.

For his part, it seems that Bonny was indeed interested in her money. While he probably found her fun and attractive, it was Anne's future inheritance that really set his heart racing. He continued to court her, hoping no doubt that her father would come around, but even when he did not, the two took their chances by eloping and running away to get married. William Cormac responded as promised and disowned her.

One legend has it that Anne was so incensed at being cut out of her father's will that she decided if she was not to have the plantation, no one would. The story claims Anne (and possibly Bonny) proceeded to sneak on to the grounds in the dark of night and tried to set fire to the fields and the house, but since there is no record of this event, it's likely either that Anne failed or never actually made the attempt.

Following their marriage, Anne and James moved to Nassau on what was then known as New Providence Island, hoping to find work there. When they arrived there, sometime between 1714 and 1718, it was a well-known haven for pirates, especially those from Britain. Over the previous century, many nations from Europe attempted to gain control of the various islands of the Caribbean, leading to competition that mostly took place on the seas and left no single nation able to enforce law and order in the area. Naturally, piracy exploded in this environment, with many pirates igniting fear across the warm tropical seas of the middle Atlantic.

Anne and her husband were arriving to New Providence Island right around the time Queen Anne's War was coming to an end. In Europe, the war was called the War of Spanish Succession, since that was the substance of the war, but in North America it was known as Queen Anne's War. Each of the major belligerents - Spain, France and England - controlled critical pieces of North America, ultimately sucking them in despite the fact they were far removed from European thrones. In North America, the hostilities focused principally on various border disputes, and the Native Americans in the region were also actively involved in the development of the conflict.

When the European nations were officially at war with each other, they used private sailors as privateers to aid their cause. Being a privateer was, in some sense, legalized piracy; a privateer was not a member of the Royal Navy but instead owned his own private ship and received a contract (called a letter of marquee) from the government to attack enemy ships during a time of war. This allowed the marquee-awarding government to place undercover ships out to war. It also, however, made the enemy wary of anything the opposing belligerent owned, and thus caused many private ships to be enveloped in the war, even the kinds of merchant ships that posed no threat and were essentially civilian targets.

The line between a privateer and a pirate was often vague. For practical purposes, there was no apparent difference, other than that a privateer was legally sanctioned by a government while a pirate was often a free rider independent of any larger organization. When it came to day-to-day activities, however, the aim of the privateer was the same as that of the pirate: to find treasure and to steal it.

Privateers were valuable during war, but they were a problem when the wars ended. Naturally, those who had been privateers kept doing what they did best even when their nations were no longer technically at war, and after years of serving as a sort of paramilitary organization for the British Crown, many former privateers had fallen into disrepute when peacetime made their sanctioned robbery illegal. Much had changed in the century since Elizabeth I had knighted Francis Drake for robbing Spanish ships; there was now too much legal trade going on with the New World to allow rogue pirate ships to interfere with the dealings. But the ultimate result was that the privateers who had once served their own nations now had no qualms about robbing from the mother country anymore.

In a letter written by Governor Hamilton, English governor of the Bahamas, to the Council of Trade on April 10, 1716, he complained:

> "In my former letter I acquainted your Lordships with Captain Soanes, H.M.S. Seahorse, who did design to leave this station and notwithstanding all the arguments that I have used, he does persist in his resolution of going home for Great Britain, before the arrival of the other ship of war to supply his place, and notwithstanding that we have now pirates among these Islands which I had an account of one of the Lieut. Governor of Antigua had been seen off for eight or ten days to the Windward part of that Island.
>
> I therefore ordered the said Soanes to cruise five days to the East part of that Island between the latitude of sixteen and eighteen who is now returned but as I understand went only a little to the South East of that Island and so came down again not without some reflections on his being sent to cruise etc. Refers to enclosure, whereby he peremptorily resolves to leave this station, by which I shall be left without a man of war and if any pirates are or should continue among these Islands, it will not only prevent my going from Island to Island as H.M. service will require me, but very dangerous to the ships trading to and from these Islands."

As a result of this and similar complaints from other governors, King George I issued the following proclamation in the summer of 1717:

> "Whereas we have received information, that several persons, subjects of great Britain, have, since the twenty fourth day of June, in the year of our Lord one thousand, seven hundred and fifteen, committed diverse piracies and robberies upon the high seas in the West Indies, or adjoining to our plantations,

which have, and may occasion, great damage to the merchants of Great Britain and others, trading into those parts; and though we have appointed such a force as we judge sufficient for suppressing the said piracies: yet the more effectually to put an end to the same, we have thought fit, by and with the advice of our privy council, to issue this our royal proclamation; and we do hereby promise and declare, that in case any of the said pirates shall, on or before the fifth day of September, in the year of our Lord one thousand, seven hundred and eighteen, surrender him or themselves to one of our principal secretaries of state in Great Britain or Ireland, or to any governor or deputy governor of any of our plantations or dominions beyond the seas, every such pirate and pirates, so surrendering him or themselves, as aforesaid, shall have our gracious pardon of and for such his or their piracy or piracies, by him or them."

George I

Among those who took advantage of the king's offer of clemency was James Bonny, who promised to give up his pirating ways and walk a straight and narrow path. In return, the Crown and its representatives agreed not to prosecute him for any past crimes he was known or discovered to be associated with. This was common practice among many pirates at that time, especially the small time ones like Bonny.

Bonny, however, took it one step further. In the summer of 1718, he offered his services to the new governor, Woodes Rogers, as an informant. It is hard to say why he chose to do this, but the most likely answer, of course, is money. Bonny had never enjoyed hard work very much, and now that he had a wife to support, he had to find some way to earn a living.

On the other hand, there may have been another, more pressing reason why he wanted to get into the new governor's good graces. Anne was pregnant, and James had reason to believe that the birth of his first grandchild might soften old William Cormac's heart toward the young couple. In order to precipitate this, James needed to show that he had changed and was ready to be a responsible husband and father. He may have hoped that, by becoming a friend of the governor, he could persuade him to put in a good word for him with his father-in-law.

Chapter 4: The Vane Mutiny

Like many other shadowy characters of the Golden Age of Piracy, little is known about Jack Rackham's early years, and in Calico Jack's case, the historical record is even emptier than usual. The only information about his origins is that he was an Englishman who was born in Cuba around 1682, and there is no record of his ancestry or what his family was like. Part of the problem in finding information about Rackham's early life is due to difficulties related to his family name. As is often the case with the pirates of that era, there are discrepancies in the spelling of his name, which is hardly surprising given that pirates frequently used aliases to help evade authorities or subject their family to problems associated with being related to a criminal. Some documents refer to him as Rackam, while others spell it Rackum.

The first written record of Rackham's life comes from the log of the *Ranger*, a sloop Captained by Charles Vane. According to Vane's records, by 1718 Rackham had risen to the rank of quartermaster under his command, making him the second highest ranked officer on the ship behind the captain himself. Based on that log, it's likely that Calico Jack had been at sea for much of the first 30 years of his life, and since men rarely went to sea after a life on land, Rackham probably began his career as a cabin boy while still in his early teens.

18th century engraving that depicts Vane

By 1718, Charles Vane was one of the New World's most notorious pirates, and he had become famous for his success against Spanish galleons trying to safely move gold across the Gulf of Mexico. On a more personal level, Vane's name had become associated with torturing and murdering the crews he caught, cheating his own men out of booty, and mercilessly attacking any target he felt emboldened enough to take, including a 12-gun brigantine that he christened the *Ranger*.

Given his past, most historians believe that Vane and his shipmates (likely including Calico Jack) were initially English privateers, and Vane was at the height of his career in the beginning of 1718 when the King offered pardons to any pirates who would surrender themselves and promise to give up piracy. Before the pardon was offered by the King, Vane's crew had spent much of their time on shore at New Providence, a once uninhabited island that privateer-turned-pirate Henry Jennings helped turn into a lawless trading town consisting mostly of pirates and other traders. The island was the perfect spot for pirates because it was close to the commercial shipping lanes near Florida Strait, it was big enough for dozens of ships to dock, and it was shallow enough that the various imperial navies of the European empires had to avoid giving chase too far. Author George Woodbury noted New Providence was "a place of temporary sojourn and refreshment for a literally floating population," and that its residents "were the piratical camp followers, the traders, and the hangers-on…", which he renamed the Ranger. According to legend, Vane had nearly been captured by a Royal Navy ship, the HMS *Phoenix*, in early 1718, and he was able to talk his way out of capture by claiming he was on the way to New Providence to accept the pardon. Once his freedom was secured, he ignored his own lie and went back to piracy.

At the king's behest, Captain Woodes Rogers traveled to the West Indies to become governor of New Providence, and one of the goals of his governorship was to convince as many pirates as possible to accept the pardons, which would help him clean up New Providence that much faster. Rogers was backed up by two British men-of-war, which induced many pirates with lesser ships to take the pardon, but Rackham and the rest of Vane's crew refused the offer, preferring to take their chances on the open seas. In fact, Vane was so defiant that he had the *Ranger* fire at Rogers' ship as the pirate and his crew left the island.

Ironically, the pirates who accepted pardons were now put to use trying to capture the pirates who refused the offer, and many former pirates found it more lucrative to go after other pirates instead of merchant ships. As wanted men, Vane and his crew began sailing up and down the Eastern coast of the North America, hoping to trap ships sailing to or from England with supplies for the American colonies. In October, Vane and the crew even barely escaped capture and managed to spend a week off the coast of North Carolina with the most famous pirate of them all. The anonymous author writing under the pseudonym Captain Charles Johnson explained:

> "Vane cruised some Time off the Bar, in hopes to catch Yeats at his coming out again, but therein he was disappointed; however, he unfortunately for them, took two Ships from Charles-Town, bound home to England. It happen'd that just at this Time two Sloops well mann'd and arm'd, were equipp'd to go after a Pyrate, which the Governor of South-Carolina was informed, lay then in Cape Fear River, a cleaning: But Colonel Rhet, who commanded the Sloops, meeting with one of the Ships that Vane had plundered, going back over the Bar, for such Necessaries as had been taken from her, and she giving the Colonel an Account of her being taken by the Pyrate Vane, and also, that some of her Men, while they were Prisoners on Board of him, had heard the Pyrates say, they should clean in one of the Rivers to the Southward; he altered his first Design, and instead of standing to the Northward, in pursuit of the Pyrate in Cape Fear River, he turns to the Southward after Vane; who had ordered such Reports to be given out, on purpose to send any Force that should come after him, upon a wrong Scent; for in Reality he stood away to the Northward, so that the Pursuit proved to be the contrary Way.
>
> Colonel Rhet's speaking with this Ship, was the most unlucky Thing that could have happened, because it turned him out of the Road, which in all Probability, would have brought him into the Company of Vane, as well as of the Pyrate he went after; and so

they might have been both destroy'd; whereas, by the Colonel's going a different Way, he not only lost the Opportunity of meeting with one, but if the other had not been infatuated, to lye six Weeks together at Cape Fear, he would have missed of him likewise: However, the Colonel having searched the Rivers and Inlets, as directed, for several Days, without Success, at length sailed in Prosecution of his first Design, and met with the Pyrate accordingly, whom he fought and took, as has been before spoken of, in the History of Major Bonnet.

Captain Vane went into an Inlet to the Northward, where he met with Captain Thatch, or Teach, otherwise call'd Black-beard, whom he saluted (when he found who he was) with his great Guns, loaded with Shot, (as is the Custom among Pyrates when they meet) which are fired wide, or up into the Air: Black-beard answered the Salute in the same Manner, and mutual Civilities passed for some Days; when about the Beginning of October, Vane took Leave, and sailed further to the Northward."

By this time, however, Vane's personality and discord among some of his shipmates resulted in one of his two pirate ships taking off without him:

"For Captain Vane, having always treated his Consort with very little Respect, assuming a Superiority over Yeats and his small Crew, and regarding the Vessel but as a Tender to his own; gave them a Disgust, who thought themselves as good Pyrates, and as great Rogues as the best of them; so they caball'd together, and resolved to take the first Opportunity to leave the Company; and accept of his Majesty's Pardon, or set up for themselves, either of which they thought more honourable than to be Servants to the former; and the putting aboard so many Negroes, where they found so few Hands to take Care of them, still aggravated the Matter, though they thought fit to conceal or stifle their Resentments at that Time.

A Day or two afterwards, the Pyrates lying off at Anchor, Yeats in the Evening slipp'd his Cable, and put his Vessel under Sail, standing into the Shore; which, when Vane saw, he was highly provoked, and got his Sloop under Sail to chase his Consort, who, he plainly perceived, had a Mind to have no further Affairs with him: Vane's Brigantine sailing best, he gained Ground of Yeats, and would certainly have come up with him, had he had a little longer Run for it; but just as he got over the Bar, when Vane came within Gun-shot of him, he fired a Broadside at his old Friend, (which did him no Damage,) and so took his Leave."

Now reduced to one ship, the crew of the *Ranger* encountered several ships along the coast of New York and attacked and plundered them, but on November 24, 1718, Vane and his crew sighted a ship and hoisted their pirate flag, figuring it would be enough to compel the target to surrender. They were greatly surprised when the ship instead hoisted colors that indicated it was a French man-of-war and fired a broadside at the *Ranger*. It was one of the largest ships the pirates had ever seen, and more than twice as large as the *Ranger*. Seeing how well it was armed, Vane thought it best to give the larger vessel a wide berth and stay out of her way, so he ordered his men to retreat where they would not be noticed and could avoid being attacked.

It was at this point that Calico Jack began making his mark on the Golden Age of Piracy. In opposition to Vane's plan, Rackham spoke up in favor of attacking, claiming he saw no reason not to attack and capture the larger ship. The pirates had a pattern of "trading up" to better ships by capturing them, and Rackham rightly pointed out that the huge French ship would likely be loaded with valuable cargo and could be a ship to use for future piracy. When Vane disagreed, Rackham told other members of the crew about his opinion, and most of the 90 pirates agreed with him, leading to a mutiny.

According to one historian:

"During this Chace, the Pyrates were divided in their Resolutions what to do: *Vane*, the Captain, was for making off as fast as he could, alledging the Man of War was too strong to cope with; but one *John Rackam*, who was an Officer, that had a kind of a Check upon the Captain, rose up in Defence of a contrary Opinion, saying, *That tho' she had more Guns, and a greater Weight of Mettal, they might board her, and then the best Boys would carry the Day. Rackam* was well seconded, and the Majority was for boarding; but *Vane* urged, *That it was too rash and desperate an Enterprize, the Man of War appearing to be twice their Force; and that their Brigantine might be sunk by her before they could reach on board.* The Mate, one *Robert Deal*, was of *Vane*'s Opinion, as were about fifteen more, and all the rest joined with *Rackam*, the Quarter-Master. At length the Captain made use of his Power to determine this Dispute, which, in these Cases, is absolute and uncontroulable, by their own Laws, *viz.* in *fighting, chasing*, or *being chased*; in all other Matters whatsoever, he is governed by a Majority; so the Brigantine having the Heels, as they term it, of the *French* Man, she came clear off.

But the next Day, the Captain's Behaviour was obliged to stand the Test of a Vote, and a Resolution passed against his Honour and Dignity, branding him with the Name of Coward, deposing him from the Command, and turning him out of the Company, with Marks of Infamy; and, with him, went all those who did not Vote for boarding the *French* Man of War. They had with them a small Sloop that had been taken by them some Time before, which they gave to *Vane*, and the discarded Members; and, that they might be in a Condition to provide for themselves, by their own honest Endeavours, they let them have a sufficient Quantity of Provisions and Ammunition along with them."

According to the records, Rackham set Vane and the fifteen men who had supported him afloat on the sloop, rather than killing them as many other mutineers had in the past. They even provided their former crewmates with enough food to survive and ammunition to defend themselves. Vane would eventually find his way back to piracy, but now Calico Jack was in charge.

Chapter 5: Captain Rackham

Following his rise to the captaincy, Rackham got off to a good start after sailing toward the Leeward Islands, where he and his crew of about 75 pirates captured several ships and plundered their cargo. Among those captured was a tavern keeper named Hosea Tisdall from Jamaica who pleaded with Rackham to allow him to return to his home. For whatever reason, Rackham agreed to their request, and as they made their way toward Jamaica, the *Ranger* captured a ship sailing from Madera, holding the captain for several days while plundering the ship. When they returned the ship to him, they allowed Tisdall to go with him so that he could make his way back to Jamaica. Rackham and the crew then proceeded on their way.

By this time it was nearly the end of the year, and the men were anxious for a break, so Rackham ordered them to drop anchor at a small island near Jamaica. There the pirates celebrated Christmas on shore, and they took advantage of their break by spending most of their time drinking, sleeping and chasing women. When they ran out of liquor and sobered up, they devoted the rest of their time to cleaning and repairing their ship. Captain Charles Johnson explained what prompted them to head back to sea: "After this Cruize, they went into a small Island and cleaned, and spent their Christmas ashore, drinking and carousing as long as they had any Liquor left, and then went to Sea again for more."

Though they sailed around the Caribbean for more than two months, Calico Jack and his crew did not have much luck in their pursuits. In fact, the only ship they ran into was a ship carrying criminals from the English prison at Newgate to work on the plantations being established in America. They kept the ship for a while, trying to decide what to do with her and her cargo, but before they reached a decision an English man-of-war approached, forcing them to turn the ship loose and make their own escape.

After finding little to interest them around Jamaica, Rackham and his crew made their way toward Bermuda, and along the way they captured a ship that had recently left the Carolinas and another ship sailing from New England. They took both ships to the Bahamas, where they cleaned and repaired both of them and the *Ranger*, after which they restocked all the ships and refitted them for a new voyage.

Calico Jack might have had 3 ships with which to prey on his targets, but apparently the pirates tarried in the Bahamas too long, because Captain Woodes Rogers, the governor of New Providence, got news of their presence there and sent a ship to capture them. The pirates managed to spot the English sloop far off shore, and after seeing that it appeared to be both well-armed and well-manned, the pirates decided to make a run for it. To ensure a speedy escape, they had to sacrifice the two prizes they had previously taken, and once again they only had the

Ranger.

By the time Calico Jack and his pirates left shore, they had established something of a routine in the way they lived; they would sail around the Caribbean for a few months looking for ships to seize before returning to the island of Cuba, where many had unofficial families. One of those men was Rackham himself, who apparently had a common law wife and perhaps even a child or two living there. Thus, when the pirates left the Bahamas, they decided to return to Cuba and spend the booty they had taken before they abandoned the other ships.

Feeling safe on the large island, Calico Jack and his crew remained in Cuba for several months, spending most of their newly gained treasure on "wine, women and song." They also completed the work they had begun on the *Ranger* back in the Bahamas, and they were preparing to return to sea when their plans were interrupted by a man-of-war sailing toward Cuba's coast with a captured English sloop in tow. Seeing the pirates, the ship attacked, but before they could defeat the *Ranger* Calico Jack managed to sail into the shallower waters of a nearby island, where the larger ship could not safely follow them.

Unwilling to give up her potential prize so easily, the man-of-war sailed into the channel and dropped anchor, determined to wait until Rackham tried to make a run for it. Through his spy glass, Rackham could easily see his enemy, and the captain discussed the situation with his men to choose how the pirate ship would proceed. After much discussion, they came up with a plan that was both elegant in its simplicity and cunning in its execution. In the dark of the moonless night, Rackham sailed the *Ranger* up to the English sloop being towed in by the man-of-war and silently boarded her, getting the jump on the few sleeping Spaniards who were supposed to be guarding the sloop. The pirates woke each Spaniard by placing a knife to his throat and whispering that if he made so much as a sound, it would be his last. Within moments, Rackham and his men had complete possession of the English sloop that was being towed in by the man-of-war, and they quickly untied her from her Spanish captor and sailed her into open waters, leaving behind the tired old *Ranger* in her stead.

It was not until daylight that the men on the man-of-war realized what had happened, and they furiously fired on the *Ranger* hoping to kill anyone left aboard. Of course, the *Ranger* was empty, and her former crew had already disappeared past the horizon in a newer and faster ship. The man-of-war was thus left with only a now bullet riddled hull of an empty ship for their prize.

One of the things that enabled Rackham to move so quickly and silently against the man-of-war and its captured sloop was that his crew was significantly smaller than it had been in the past. Many of his men had chosen to stay behind in Cuba, so Rackham found himself sailing about the Caribbean with something resembling a skeleton crew. Nevertheless, as he sailed toward Jamaica, perhaps in hopes of recruiting more men, along the way he was able to attack and plunder several smaller vessels. While the booty on board provided the pirates with food and drink, Calico Jack and his crew had reached a breaking point; either he had to add to the crew or change his ways.

Chapter 6: Anne Bonny and Mary Read

Sometime in 1719, Calico Jack made his way back to Jamaica to add to his crew, and he would end up meeting one of the most famous pirates in history while he was there. During his stay in Jamaica, Rackham met a Frenchman named Pierre, who ran a popular salon that was frequented by the ladies of the island. One of those ladies was a young woman named Anne Bonny, the daughter of a prominent New World businessman. She was in her late teens but had already been married to James Bonny, a one-time pirate who had taken the pardon offer and was now a sailor for the Jamaican governor.

Although Anne Bonny may have been pregnant when she met Calico Jack, she was still young and pretty, and she had became bored with her life as the wife of a poor seaman. She found herself missing the social life that her father's home provided, but she was also too proud to return home and instead frequented the local pub for companionship instead. Little is known about Calico Jack's looks or his demeanor, but there was something about him that attracted young Anne. However, there was the delicate matter of her child and her husband. With Pierre's help, she found a place to live until she had her child, but as soon as she recovered from the birth, she left the boy with his father and took off to meet Rackham.

18th century engraving depicting Anne Bonny

In the early months of 1719, Anne, Calico Jack, and the rest of his crew sailed around the islands of the Bahamas, doing some minor pilfering and harassing local vessels. It's been alleged that Anne dressed up as a man as part of the crew, but it's unclear whether this is true, and after a few months Anne found herself pregnant again. When she shared the news with Rackham, he was not particularly pleased, since he enjoyed having her for a mistress but had no interest in being a father. Since she was not exactly the maternal type either, the two made a plan to deal with their unwanted pregnancy. When Anne's pregnancy would render her unfit for piracy, Calico Jack took her to Cuba and arranged for Anne to stay with his "Cuban family" until her child was delivered. He returned a few months later, picking Anne up from the island and leaving the child behind to be cared for, most likely with his half-siblings, by Rackham's former mistress. Rumor has it that he was later adopted by an English family by the name of Cunningham. What is clear, however, is that the child never saw either of his parents again.

Once she had recovered from childbirth, Anne returned to Rackham's ship, the *Revenge*. By this time she had been divorced by her husband, who cited abandonment for the grounds. It's also believed that Calico Jack offered to buy Anne in a "divorce by purchase," but she refused that arrangement herself. Either way, once she was divorced from Bonny, this left her free to marry Rackham, but there is no evidence that the two were ever legally wed.

As Calico Jack and his lover took to the seas once again, the King issued yet another offer of amnesty to those pirates who would turn themselves in and promise to walk the straight and narrow path of honest work. Despite the attempts of Rogers and other privateers, there was not enough success in 1718 to satisfy the Crown. Near the end of that year, on December 21, 1718, King George I issued yet another proclamation, this time reviewing his past offers of pardons and reiterating the bounty on the heads of the remaining pirates. The largest bounty was placed on Blackbeard's head, but a sizable bounty was also placed on the head of anybody else commanding a pirate ship.:

"Whereas we did think fit, by and with the advice of our privy council, to issue our royal proclamation, bearing date the fifth day of September, one thousand, seven hundred and seventeen, in the fourth year of our reign, therein taking notice, that we had received information, that several persons, subjects of Great Britain, had, since the four and twentieth day of June, in the year of our lord one thousand, seven hundred and fifteen, committed divers piracies and robberies upon the high seas in the West Indies, or adjoining to our plantations, which had and might occasion great damage to the merchants of Great Britain, and others, trading into those parts: and we did thereby promise and declare, that in case any the said pirates should, on or before the fifth day of September, one thousand, seven hundred and eighteen, surrender him or themselves in manner as therein is directed, every such pirate and pirates, so surrendering him or themselves, as aforesaid, should have our gracious pardon of and for such his or their piracy or piracies, by him or them committed before the fifth day of January then next ensuing: and whereas several of the said pirates, not having had timely notice of our said proclamation, may not have surrendered themselves within the time therein appointed, and by reason thereof are incapable of receiving the benefit of our royal mercy and clemency intended thereby: and though we have appointed such a force, as we judge sufficient for suppressing the said piracies, yet the more effectually to put an end to the same, we have thought fit, by and with the advice of our privy-council, to issue this our royal proclamation; and we do hereby promise and declare, that in case any the said pirates shall, on or before the first day of July, in the year of our lord one thousand, seven hundred and nineteen, surrender him or themselves to one of our principal secretaries of state in Great Britain or Ireland, or to any governor or deputy-governor of any of our plantations or dominions beyond the seas, every such pirate and pirates, so surrendering him or themselves, as aforesaid, shall have our gracious pardon of and for such his or their piracy or piracies, by him or them committed before such time as they shall have received notice of this our royal proclamation; which pardon or pardons we have authorized and commanded our respective governors to grant accordingly. And we do hereby strictly charge and command all our admirals, captains, and other officers at sea, and all our governors and commanders of any forts, castles, or other places in our plantations, and all others our officers civil and military, to seize and take such of the pirates, who shall refuse or neglect to surrender themselves accordingly. And we do hereby further declare, that in case any person or persons, on or after the first day of July, one thousand, seven hundred and nineteen, shall discover or seize, or cause or procure to be discovered or seized, any one or more of the said pirates, so neglecting or refusing to surrender themselves, as aforesaid, so as they may be brought to justice, and convicted of the said offence, such person or persons, so making such discovery or seizure, or causing or procuring such discovery or seizure to be made, shall have and receive as a reward for the same, (viz.) for every commander of any pirate-ship or vessel the sum of one hundred pounds; for every lieutenant, master, boatswain, carpenter, and gunner, the sum of forty pounds; for every inferior officer the sum of thirty pounds; and for every private man, the sum of twenty pounds; and if any person or persons, belonging to, and being part of the crew of any such pirate-ship or vessel, shall, on or after the said first day of July, one thousand, seven hundred and nineteen, seize and deliver, or cause to be seized and delivered, any commander or commanders of such pirate-ship or vessel, so as that he or they be brought to justice, and convicted of the said offence, such person or persons, as a reward for the same, shall receive for every such commander the sum of two hundred pounds; which said sums the lord treasurer, or the commissioners of our treasury for the time being, are hereby required and directed to pay accordingly.

Given at our court at St. James s, the twenty-first day of

December 1718. In the fifth year of our reign.

God save the king."

As a result of this bounty, hunting pirates suddenly became more lucrative than being one. After discussing the options with Anne and the rest of his crew, Rackham decided to give the honest life a try. Though he had rejected the previous pardon offer, his luck had not been too good lately, and he was ready to try something else. Calico Jack turned his ship toward the nearest fort, where he and his crew confessed to all (or at least most) of their piracy and swore to live out the rest of their days as honest sailors in the service of His Majesty.

Of course, the question arose as to how they were to make their living if not through piracy, but Rackham was one step ahead of his men. He explained that, as pirates themselves, they knew the hiding places and plans use by fellow pirates in the area. The King was offering a generous bounty for the capture of their former cohorts, so if they were no longer going to survive by being pirates, why not make their living by hunting them down?

Unfortunately, hunting pirates proved to be easier said than done. For one thing, many of the more serious captains were simply too smart to get caught. Likewise, the ones that could be easily found were few and far between. Many of them had taken the same path as Rackham and had become pirate hunters themselves. After a few months of trying to live their lives within the confines of the law, Rackham and his men gave up and returned to their former lives as pirates.

Chapter 7: Mary Read Joins the Crew

Upon heading west, it wouldn't take long for Mary to determine her new line of work. On her voyage across the Atlantic, her ship was captured by an unknown pirate ship sometime before they reached their island destination. Because Mary was the only English speaking sailor aboard that particular ship, the captain of the ship, thinking she was a man, offered her the opportunity to join his crew and become a pirate herself. Seeing the plunder that the men were taking for themselves, and the ease with which they took the ship, Mary took him up on this offer.

Mary likely traveled to the West Indies just as piracy was becoming rampant there, and it seems for the next few years she lived the life of a pirate while Calico Jack served under Vane and then captained his own ship. When the first clemency offer was made by the Crown, the pirate crew with whom Mary had been serving decided to surrender themselves and try living within the law for a change. For her part, Mary went to work back on shore, though it is unclear whether she did so as a man or woman, but before long a new sailing opportunity presented itself.

Once Calico Jack and Anne Bonny returned to piracy, Rackham lost no time in going after the next small ship he saw. During one of these voyages in 1719, Rackham came upon a moderately sized ship crewed by a bunch of men from the West Indies. After commandeering the ship, Calico Jack offered to let members of that boat join his crew, including an Englishman who he introduced to Anne. From the start Anne was fascinated by this new member of their crew, drawn to his delicately high pitched voice and clean shaven appearance. While most of the men wore beards or at least mustaches, this new man always kept his face clean shaven. As time went on, Anne found herself going out of her way to speak to him or work near him, and before long the two had become close friends.

As it turned out, the Englishman was no man at all. Like Calico Jack and Anne Bonny, Mary Read was a former pirate turned privateer, and it's unclear what choice she had but to join Rackham's crew after her ship was commandeered by the pirate. Mary would later insist that she had never intended to be a pirate but had simply fell into the life by accident, and that she only turned to the life after she was captured and forced to serve aboard a pirate ship. She further claimed that it was always her intention to abandon piracy as soon as she could. While all of that may have been possible, those statements would be made during her trial, when she was fighting for her life. Naturally, her trial was hardly the time to say that she had always wanted to be a pirate and could hardly wait to go back to it

For a time, Mary continued to keep her identity as a woman a secret from Anne, but as Anne continued to make sexual advances towards her, things were clearly complicated. Sensitive to the problems of being the new love of the captain's mistress, Mary chose to confide her true sex to Anne. According to legend, Anne did not lose her romantic interest in Mary when she found out she was a woman, and it is maintained by some that the two became lovers themselves, though initially keeping Mary's gender and their relationship a secret from Rackham.

Eventually, Calico Jack noticed his romantic rival, who he still thought was a man. As Johnson noted, "[T]his Intimacy so disturb'd Captain Rackam, who was the Lover and Gallant of Anne Bonny, that he grew furiously jealous, so that he told Anne Bonny, he would cut her new Lover's Throat…" After he had threatened to execute his rival, Anne, concerned about Mary's safety, decided to admit to Calico Jack that the other pirate was actually a woman. In a manner best left to the imagination, Rackham confirmed that this was true, and welcomed Mary to his crew and later, some say, his bed. As Johnson put it, "Captain Rackam, (as he was enjoined,) kept the Thing a Secret from all the Ship's Company, yet, notwithstanding all her Cunning and Reserve, Love found her out in this Disguise, and hinder'd her from forgetting her Sex."

It has long been speculated that the three of them all became lovers together. Whether this is true or not, the fact does remain that Mary and Anne remained very close to each during the rest of their time sailing together. But while Anne was known as the captain's woman and thus did not have to try to pass herself off as a man, Mary remained a female in hiding, living and working among the men as one of them.

Having established a pattern of almost group captaincy, Calico Jack, Anne Bonny and Mary Read began to work together to recruit more crew members, planning for long careers on the open seas. But they were doing so at a bad time; England, which had once turned a blind eye toward attacks on her enemy's vessels, was now joining with forces from other countries to hunt down pirates. Gone were the days when Grace O'Malley could meet with the queen, or when Francis Drake received a knighthood for attacking and pillaging Spanish vessels. Early 18th century Europe was colonial and business oriented. They needed safe waterways to guarantee their profits and keep tax revenue coming in from new products being brought to Europe from the Americas.

The sun was setting on the Golden Age of Piracy, and unbeknownst to them, their days of freedom were already numbered.

18th century depiction of Anne Bonny and Mary Read

Chapter 8: 1720

For the first few months of 1720, all went well for the Revenge, which continued to cruise around the coast of the Bahamas looking for ships that appeared to be transporting treasure. They would then fire a cannon ball over their bows and signal for them to surrender. Most did, and they quickly came alongside, boarded the ship and took what they wanted. Because Calico Jack still had a relatively small crew, they shied away from the biggest ships and thus never made a really big score like Black Bart or Blackbeard, and they were also not as bloodthirsty as some in their trade, typically allowing the captured crew to sail away to safety as soon as they got what they wanted.

Mary soon proved herself to be one of Calico Jack's best fighters. There are several reasons why this young woman proved to be so fierce. For one thing, Mary had had to become a good fighter in order to keep her identity secret. Homosexual relations among ships' crews were a natural occurrence given the lack of any available women, but Mary couldn't afford to potentially let the rest of the crew know she wasn't a man. Since she would definitely have been on of the most effeminate members of any crew she belonged to, she would have had to have been tough to fend off unwanted advances that might have given away her secret. Another reason for Mary's martial strength was that she had had plenty of practice defending herself through the years. She had made a living out of being a soldier, sailor, and even a member of a cavalry unit, all of which required her to be as strong and tough as the men she was serving alongside.

Similarly, according to the legends Anne was a fierce fighter and every bit as aggressive as Rackham himself. She was known to be a good shot and cool under pressure, and whenever there was a battle to be fought, she would be in the thick of it and would not quit until the job was done or the rest of the crew had decided to give up. Naturally, before long the tale of the two women pirates in Calico Jack's crew had made its way around the ships and pubs along the waterfront. Some claimed that it could not be possible that two women would be able to fight as well as men. Others, however, told a different tale. Those who had faced them in battle or fought alongside them on the *Revenge* were happy to tell tales of their exploits together.

In addition to taking each ship's cargo, the pirates were also inclined to take some of the more useful crew members. This was achieved in one of two ways. First, Calico Jack, after spotting a young man who had talents that he thought his crew could use, would approach him and suggest that he throw in his lot with them. Often the man in question would agree, and that would be that. However, some were more reluctant to give up their honest work. At this point, the pirate captain might reconsider his decision and let him remain on his own ship. But if Rackham still felt that he needed the man, he would force the man to join the crew.

Once on Calico Jack's ship, Mary had the first opportunity in her life to be who she truly was: a woman who enjoyed living her life as a man. But just as things had gotten complicated when Anne took an interest in her, things again got complicated when Mary took an interest in one of her crewmates, who had been forced into service on the *Revenge*. Before long, they were sharing the same table and slept near each other at night, igniting Mary's passions. If she made her feelings known without revealing her sex, she would obviously be misleading the other sailor, but if she did let him in on her secret and he was not interested, she would likely lose her place on the crew.

According to Johnson, Mary eventually revealed her sex to this new object of her affection, though whether it was intentional or not was unclear:

"In their Cruize they took a great Number of Ships belonging to Jamaica, and other Parts of the West-Indies, bound to and from England; and when ever they meet any good Artist, or other Person that might be of any great Use to their Company, if he was not willing to enter, it was their Custom to keep him by Force. Among these was a young Fellow of a most engageing Behaviour, or, at least, he was so in the Eyes of Mary Read, who became so smitten with his Person and Address, that she could neither rest, Night or Day; but as there is nothing more ingenious than Love, it was no hard Matter for her, who had before been practiced in these Wiles, to find a Way to let him discover her Sex: She first insinuated her self into his liking, by talking against the Life of a Pyrate, which he was altogether averse to, so they became Mess-Mates and strict Companions: When she found he had a Friendship for her, as a Man, she suffered the

Discovery to be made, by carelesly shewing her Breasts, which were very White. The young Fellow, who was made of Flesh and Blood, had his Curiosity and Desire so rais'd by this Sight, that he never ceased importuning her, till she confessed what she was."

After Mary admitted she was a woman, the two soon became lovers, though they kept their relationship a secret for both of their sakes. On the one hand, Mary wanted to remain known as a man. On the other, she made it clear that Calico Jack would not take it well if he discovered she was involved with another man.

For a while, they were able to keep their love a secret, but the young man still did not like the life of a pirate and was not settling in well with the crew. Before long, he so angered one of his fellow crew members that the man challenged him to a duel. Young and cocky, Mary's lover agreed and they planned to meet on the next island the ship stopped at. When they dropped anchor near one of the smaller islands in the West Indies, the men agreed to go ashore the next day and settle their quarrel.

Mary was obviously concerned about the fate of the man. While she could not stand the idea of him sacrificing his pride by refusing the challenge, she still hated to see him risk his life. In perhaps the most famous legend of Mary Read's life, she devised a clever way to intervene on his behalf herself. Because the crew still thought she was a man, she decided to pick her own fight with the man her lover was set to duel, going out of her way to offend him until he finally had enough and threatened her. In order to protect her lover's safety, Mary made sure that her own duel with the man came a few hours before he was set to duel her lover.

It has long been speculated that Captain Charles Johnson, the author of the pirate history, was a pirate himself, and the manner in which he described Mary Read's duel with this pirate certainly suggests he found the violence romantic:

"[H]er Passion was no less violent than his, and perhaps she express'd it, by one of the most generous Actions that ever Love inspired. It happened this young Fellow had a Quarrel with one of the Pyrates, and their Ship then lying at an Anchor, near one of the Islands, they had appointed to go ashore and fight, according to the Custom of the Pyrates: Mary Read, was to the last Degree uneasy and anxious, for the Fate of her Lover; she would not have had him refuse the Challenge, because, she could not bear the Thoughts of his being branded with Cowardise; on the other Side, she dreaded the Event, and apprehended the Fellow might be too hard for him: When Love once enters into the Breast of one who has any Sparks of Generosity, it stirs the Heart up to the most noble Actions; in this Dilemma, she shew'd, that she fear'd more for his Life than she did for her own; for she took a Resolution of quarreling with this Fellow her self, and having challenged him ashore, she appointed the Time two Hours sooner than that when he was to meet her Lover, where she fought him at Sword and Pistol, and killed him upon the Spot.

It is true, she had fought before, when she had been insulted by some of those Fellows, but now it was altogether in her Lover's Cause, she stood as it were betwixt him and Death, as if she could not live without him. If he had no regard for her before, this Action would have bound him to her for ever; but there was no Occasion for Ties or Obligations, his Inclination towards her was sufficient; in fine, they applied their Troth to each other, which Mary Read said, she look'd upon to be as good a Marriage, in Conscience, as if it had been done by a Minister in Church; and to this was owing her great Belly, which she pleaded to save her Life."

Indeed, Mary's actions eventually made her lover even fonder of her, but time was running out on the pirates. Months before they were ultimately captured, Calico Jack's crew were nearly captured, only to turn the tables in a daring plot. Captain Charles Johnson explained how the pirates captured one of their biggest prizes:

"They repaired to their Vessel, and was making ready to put Sea, when a Guarda del Costa came in with a small English Sloop, which she had taken as an Interloper on the Coast. The Spanish Guardship attack'd the Pyrate, but Rackam being close in behind a little Island, she could do but little Execution where she lay, therefore the Spaniard warps into the Channel that Evening, in order to make sure of her the next Morning. Rackam finding his Case desperate, and hardly any Possibility of escaping, resolved to attempt the following Enterprize: The Spanish Prize lying for better Security close into the Land, between the little Island and the Main; Rackam takes his Crew into the Boat, with their Pistols and Cutlashes, rounds the little Island, and falls aboard their Prize silently in the dead of the Night, without being discovered, telling the Spaniards that were aboard of her, that if they spoke a Word, or made the least Noise, they were dead Men, and so became Master of her; when this was done, he slipt her Cable, and drove out to Sea: The Spanish Man of War, was so intent upon their expected Prize, that they minded nothing else, and as soon as Day broke, made a furious Fire upon the empty Sloop, but it was not long before they were rightly apprized of the Matter, and cursed themselves for Fools, to be bit out of a good rich Prize, as she prov'd to be, and to have nothing but an old crazy Hull in the room of her.

Rackam and his Crew had no Occasion to be displeased at the Exchange, that enabled them to continue some Time longer in a Way of Life that suited their depraved Tempers."

In addition to taking each ship's cargo, the pirates were also inclined to take some of the more useful crew members. This was achieved in one of two ways. First, Calico Jack, after spotting a young man who had talents that he thought his crew could use, would approach him and suggest that he throw in his lot with them. Often the man in question would agree, and that would be that. However, some were more reluctant to give up their honest work. At this point, Rackham might reconsider his decision and let him remain on his own ship, but if he still felt that he needed the man, he would simply force the man to join the crew.

Over time, the men of Rackham's crew were quite aware that they had the dubious distinction of sailing alongside one of the only female pirates in the world in Anne Bonny. Though Mary continued to wear men's clothing, Anne would dress in either a feminine or a masculine style depending on how her mood and tasks for the day dictated. She had no fear of harassment, since Rackham made it clear that she was his mistress and therefore under his protection. Of course, Anne was also perfectly capable of taking care of herself, and it is unlikely that Rackham had to rise to her defense very often. At the same time, with Anne Bonny aboard his ship, the tales of Calico Jack and his female crew member were soon making their way through all the seaside pubs on both sides of the Atlantic. Some men refused to believe it was even true, while others maintained that there was no way a woman could work the sails and fight as well as men. However, those who would end up facing Anne Bonny and Mary Read in battle would tell a different story in 1720.

Seafaring superstition at that time maintained that it was unlucky to have a woman aboard a ship, and two women would have been twice as bad. While it is obvious that such superstitions were simply products of the male dominated nature of sea life during the 18th century, it didn't seem to faze Calico Jack. If Rackham ever felt embarrassed or awkward about his relationship with Bonny and Read, he mentioned it to no one, and he seems to have been secure enough in his own masculinity to not be troubled by what others thought. Calico Jack had likely spent decades at sea already, and if someone challenged his personal toughness, chances are that they would carry away more than a bruise or two to remind them not to ask again.

The crew also had similar success in September 1720, taking more booty and increasing the size of their crew at the same time. In early September, 1720, Rackham and his crew captured about eight small fishing boats near Harbour Island. These boats carried little of value accept their nets and fishing tackle, but the sale of these items did give the small crew enough capital to finance a trip to French Hispaniola. There they dropped anchor and went ashore looking for what they might steal, but all they found were some cattle roaming through the woods. They brought these on board, as well as several Frenchmen who were on the island hunting wild boar.

From Hispaniola, the small band made their way back to Jamaica, managing to plunder two more sloops while on their way. There, near Porto Maria Bay, they captured a schooner, captained by Thomas Spenlow, on October 19. The following morning, Rackham spotted another sloop, this one in dry dock near the coast. He fired a shot into the air, causing those who were working on her to run to the shore to see what was going on. While they were doing this, his own men slipped aboard and plundered the ship where it stood. When the men finally made it back to the sloop, they realized what had happened. With nothing left to work with, they sent word to Rackham that they knew they were beaten and would be just as happy to join his crew. Always in the market for new men, he accepted their offer and brought them aboard.

However, a month later, the *Revenge* was on a normal sailing expedition of the coast of Jamaica when their luck finally ran out. Unaware that he was being chased, Rackham sailed his ship hear Point Negril in the Bahamas. There he saw a small Pettiauger and went after it. Seeing that she was being chased, the Pettiauger ran ashore and landed her crew. They then hailed Rackham, and indicated by the flags that they were English. Recognizing his fellow countrymen, Rackham invited the men aboard for a drink. They agreed, and nine men joined him for beer and talk well into the night. By the time all was said and done, all the men on the ship were passed out from a combination of liquor and exhaustion.

The following morning, Mary, Anne and Calico Jack were on deck, perhaps talking or making plans for their next attack. Captain Charles Johnson explained:

> "Rackam's coasting the Island in this Manner, proved fatal to him, for Intelligence came to the Governor, of his Expedition, by a Canoa which he had surprized ashore, in Ocho Bay; upon which a Sloop was immediately fitted out, and sent round the Island in quest of him, commanded by Captain Barnet, with a good Number of Hands. Rackam rounding the Island, and drawing near the Westermost Point, called Point Negril, saw a small Pettiauger, which at sight of the Sloop, run ashore and landed her Men; when one of them hailed her, Answer was made, They were English Men, and desired the Pettiauger's Men to come on Board, and drink a Bowl of Punch, which they were prevailed upon to do; accordingly the Company came all aboard of the Pyrate, consisting of nine Persons, in an ill Hour; they were armed with Muskets and Cutlashes, but, what was their real Design by so doing, I shall not take upon me to say; but they had no sooner laid down their Arms, and taken up their Pipes, but Barnet's Sloop, which was in Pursuit of Rackam's, came in Sight."

As always, the three were on alert for the sight of any other ships in the area, so when they saw a sloop approaching off their bow, they immediately sat up and took notice. As it got closer, Rackham pulled out his spy glass and took a look. That's when he saw the flag of the Governor of Jamaica flying stiffly in the breeze. The three immediately sprang into action, changing the sails and trying to make a speedy getaway. At first it seemed that they might avoid the other ship and perhaps slip by unnoticed, but before long they realized that they were spotted and the ship was giving chase.

Rackham called for all hands on deck, but nothing happened. He then sent Mary down to the hull to rouse the men, but she had little luck as they were all still pretty drunk. Returning to Anne and Calico Jack, she reported that it looked like the men were in no condition to fight. Their only option appeared to be to outrun the other ship. For the next few hours, the three tried with all their might to escape, steering and adjusting the rigging to make the maximum use of whatever wind there was. However, they soon realized that it was futile and prepared to fight.

Anne went below decks and tried herself to rouse the sleeping pirates. Again they ignored her or gave only lip service to coming upstairs. Things changed, however, when the first cannon ball flew over the bow of the ship and splashed in the water nearby. Rackham returned fire and the battle began in earnest. Some of the crew began to stumble up the stairs of the ship, squinting in the bright sunlight and asking what was going on.

Rackham gave them a quick rundown of the situation. No doubt reminding them that, if they were captured, many if not all of them would hang. This stirred up some interest among the crew, but they were still not in any physical condition to put up a serious fight. That left Rackham, Mary and Anne to fight off the ship alone. At first it seemed they might win. However, the final blow came when the sloop put a cannon ball through the hull of the *Revenge*, causing her to begin to take on water.

The roar of sea water rushing in and the spray of salt water on their faces soon roused the rest of the crew. By then, however, it was too late for them to fight. Instead, they focused their attention on trying to stop the ship from sinking. Some men tried to wrestle a patch into place to cover up the hole while others manned the pumps, desperately trying to return the water to the sea where it belonged.

Meanwhile, the captain and women were left on the upper decks, fighting the men boarding the ship alone. Many would later testify that the women were the fiercest fighters in this battle, and that they did more damage than any of the men of the crew. However, it soon became clear that they were outnumbered, outgunned and beaten. Rackham was forced to surrender his ship and his crew to Captain Jonathan Barnet, a privateer commissioned by the Governor of Jamaica to hunt down and capture pirates.

While that description of the fighting makes for a romantic and interesting story, it is doubtful that it actually went down that way. For one thing, it is unlikely that anyone would hide below decks of a ship taking on water. Indeed, the men may very well have been below trying to repair the hole or man the pumps. The women, with less physical strength, would have remained on the deck to carry on the fight. Once the ship was boarded, they would certainly have kept on fighting, even hand to hand if necessary.

No matter how the battle may have been fought, it certainly ended with the *Revenge* and her entire crew being captured by Barnet, who shipped them off to confinement at Spanish Town, Jamaica.

Chapter 9: Trials

Not surprisingly, when the infamous crew arrived at St. Jago de la Vega in Jamaica, they attracted more than their fair share of attention. Word soon spread around the community that the famous Calico Jack had been captured and that he did in fact have women in his crew. The guards in front of the fort were soon greeted by more than one curious face, arriving at the gate in the hopes of catching a glimpse of a member of this strange crew. At some point in time, either on their way to Spanish Town, or shortly after their arrival, it became known that Mary was actually a woman. Whether she was exposed by someone else or confessed it herself is unclear, but records indicate she and Anne were segregated from the men as soon as they arrived at Spanish Town.

Those hoping to see Bonny and Read stand trial would have to wait, because Calico Jack and his male crew members were tried first. On November 16, 1720, the Admiralty Court was called into session. The charges against them, specifically numerous counts of piracy, were read aloud, and the men were given a chance to enter their pleas. Though they pled not guilty, Captain Charles Johnson recorded that "they were all Guilty of the Pyracy and Felony they were charged with, which was, the going over with a pyratical and felonious Intent to John Rackam, &c. then notorious Pyrates, and by them known to be so, they all received Sentence of Death…" There was little doubt in anyone's mind that Calico Jack and his men had indeed done everything they were accused of.

The aptly named Sir Nicholas Laws presided over the court, which quickly found Rackham guilty as charged. They also convicted the ship's Master, George Fetherston, and her quartermaster, Richard Corner, as well as six crew men who had been with Rackham for the longest time: John Davis, John Howell, Patrick Carty, Thomas Earl, James Dobbin and Noah Harwood. Rackham, Fehterston, Corner, Davis and Howell were immediately sentenced to be executed the following day.

When asked if he had a last request, Rackham asked only to see Anne one more time. Unfortunately for him, he found his lover to be little comfort in the final hours of his life. According to tradition, she is said to have told him that she was sorry to see him in such a predicament, but that "if he had fought like a Man, he need not have been hanged like a dog." With those words ringing in his ears, he was carried off to the gallows and hanged in November 1720. To send a message, the authorities had Calico Jack's body gibbeted on a small islet near the entrance to Port Royal. There they remain for the next several years, their rotting corpses gruesome warnings to other who might consider entering the pirating life. However, Calico Jack had the last laugh. Today, the point in Port Royal where his body was hanged in disgrace is known as Rackham City.

The other four men who were convicted with Rackham were executed a few days later before the court recessed until after the Christmas holidays. The next group of nine pirates was tried on

January 24, 1721, and this particular group of sailors had come on the ship when they captured their last sloop. The prosecution offered only the flimsiest of evidence against them, saying:

"That the Prisoners at the Bar, viz. John Eaton, Edward Warner, Thomas Baker, Thomas Quick, John Cole, Benjamin Palmer, Walter Rouse, John Hanson, and John Howard, came aboard the Pyrate's Sloop at Negril Point, Rackam sending his Canoe ashore for that Purpose: That they brought Guns and Cutlashes on Board with them: That when Captain Barnet chased them, some were drinking, and others walking the Deck: That there was a great Gun and a small Arm fired by the Pyrate Sloop, at Captain Barnet's Sloop, when he chased her; and that when Captain Barnet's Sloop fired at Rackam's Sloop, the Prisoners at the Bar went down under Deck. That during the Time Captain Barnet chased them, some of the Prisoners at the Bar (but which of them he could not tell) helped to row the Sloop, in order to escape from Barnet: That they all seemed to be consorted together."

The men responded to the charges with a rather clever defense:

'That they had no Witnesses: That they had bought a Pettiauger in order to go a Turtleing; and being at Negril Point, and just got ashore, they saw a Sloop with a white Pendant coming towards them, upon which they took their Arms, and hid themselves in the Bushes: That one of them hail'd the Sloop, who answer'd, They were English Men, and desired them to come aboard and drink a Bowl of Punch; which they at first refused, but afterwards with much perswasion, they went on Board, in the Sloop's Canoe, and left their own Pettiauger at Anchor: That they had been but a short Time on Board, when Captain Barnet's Sloop heaved in Sight: That Rackam ordered them to help to weigh the Sloop's Anchor immediately, which they all refused: That Rackam used violent Means to oblige them; and that when Captain Barnet came up with them, they all readily and willingly submitted.

Next, two Frenchmen gave evidence on their behalf. This concluded the evidence against them, and the jury retired to consider what they had heard. In the end, this second group of men were also convicted and sentenced to execution. Some historians would later argue that this sentence appeared to have been a bit excessive, especially since there was so little substantive evidence against them. Nonetheless, Eaton, Quick, and Baker were all hanged on February 17 and Cole, Howard and Palmer followed them to the gallows the next day. It appears, however, that the rest of the male crew members survived their trials, though little is known of the rest of their lives.

Anne and Mary were tried last of all. When called to the stand, Mary swore that she had never wanted to be a pirate, that she had only come aboard Calico Jack's ship because he kidnapped her, and that she never fought against anyone. In addition to piracy, she was charged with sexual misconduct, a charge that suggests it was obvious she was pregnant. While she could not deny her condition, she did deny that she was a fornicator or adulteress. Instead, she maintained that she was actually married to the crewman who had fathered her child. However, when she was asked to give his name, she refused, saying only that the two of them hated the pirating life and had planned to leave the ship at the earliest possibility. She went on to try to convince the Justice of the Court that they already had plans for earning an honest living on land.

Meanwhile, Anne's father had heard of her capture and began to work to get her freed. He was still a prominent planter and had several friends in Jamaica on whom he called for help. He may have even found someone to speak on his daughter's behalf to the governor. However, it proved to be of little avail against the testimony of how Anne had conducted herself while on board, and especially during the final battle with Barnet's men

Unfortunately for Anne and Mary, the testimony of some of their crewmates sunk them, especially Mary's assertion that she did not want to continue in piracy. Several men, all of whom claimed to have been kidnapped themselves, swore that during battle no one fought as hard as Mary Read or Anne Bonny. At least one of them mentioned an occasion when the women not only refused to join the men in hiding below decks but also taunted the men for refusing to join them. It was also suggested that Mary even went below decks and threatened the men there with a loaded gun, and that when the men failed to move fast enough for her, she fired on them, killing one man and wounding several others.

According to one witness, when Barnet and his men attempted to board the ship, "the two women, prisoners at the bar, were then on board the said sloop, and wore men's jackets, and long trousers, and handkerchiefs tied about their heads; and that each of them had a machete and pistol in their hands, and cursed and swore at the men, to murder the deponent; and that they should kill her, to prevent her coming against them; and the deponent further said, that the reason of her knowing and believing them to be women then was by the largeness of their breasts."

Another witness said "that when they saw any vessel, gave chase, or attacked, they wore men's clothes; and at other times, they wore woman's clothes." This, of course, calls into question whether or not Mary actually concealed her identity as well as she is believed to have, but by now it was a moot point.

According to one historian, the most damning evidence against Mary actually came from a man she had once sailed with. One of the men who claimed to have been kidnapped by Rackham and forced into piracy said that he had often had conversations with Mary about how she came to be involved in piracy. He claimed that he was curious as to why anyone would pursue a life that was so filled with dangers and discomfort. He also testified that he sought her feelings about the possibility of dying in disgrace, either at the hands of the crown, or one of her enemies. According to this man's testimony, Mary replied to his question by answering:

"as to hanging, she thought it no great Hardship, for, were it not for that, every cowardly Fellow would turn Pyrate, and so infest the Seas, that Men of Courage must starve:— That if it was put to the Choice of the Pyrates, they would not have the punishment less than Death, the Fear of which, kept some dastardly Rogues honest; that many of those who are now cheating the Widows and Orphans, and oppressing their poor Neighbours, who have no Money to obtain Justice, would then rob at Sea, and the Ocean would be crowded with Rogues, like the Land, and no Merchant would venture out; so that the Trade, in a little Time, would not be worth following."

The court thus handed down the most dreaded sentence possible to both women, declaring:

"You, Mary Read, and Ann Bonny, alias Bonn, are to go from hence to the place from whence you came, and from thence to the place of execution; where you shall be severally hanged by the neck till you are severally dead. And god of his infinite mercy be merciful to both your souls."

At this point, the judge asked the women if they had anything to say for themselves. Both came forward and asked that their sentences be delayed because they were pregnant, since English law at that time forbade the execution of pregnant women to avoid killing their unborn child as well. Whether it was obvious they were pregnant or it was something that the court had to wait to confirm is unknown, but the judge decided to grant both women a stay of execution until they delivered their babies.

Mary did not live long enough to face either the gallows or childbirth, instead dying of some sort fever in early 1721. By this time she was so far along in her pregnancy that she either delivered the child right before her death or the doctors tried to save the child by delivering it through a quick caesarean section. Either way, they both died but were buried separately in St. Catherine parish in Jamaica. Ironically, the convicted criminal and the innocent child were among the first few people to be buried in that cemetery.

Pleading the belly ultimately proved to be useless to Mary Read, but it is widely believed the delay was enough to save Anne's life. While she remained in prison awaiting her child's birth, her father continued to speak to his friends on her behalf, and eventually he was able to arrange enough bribes to enough people to secure her release. Shortly after the birth of her baby, she disappeared from the history books, probably much to the relief of authorities who had no stomach for executing a woman with an infant child.

It remains unclear as to what exactly happened to Anne after her time in prison. Some believe that she returned to James Bonny and lived out the rest of her days as his wife, but that seems unlikely. For one thing, the two of them had been legally divorced, so it is likely that he had by this time married someone else. Also, Anne's father likely felt that he had put too much effort into her release to have her return to someone he had never cared much for anyway.

Others say that she returned to being a pirate, changing her name and joining another crew, but this seems even less likely. Unlike Mary Read, Anne Bonny never showed any particular love for life at sea. Her affection centered on Calico Jack, and it seems she did what she did just so she could be with him, simply following his path.

The final possibility is that which had the only documentary evidence to support it. According to records preserved by those claiming to be her descendants, Anne and her child returned with her father to Charleston, South Carolina, sailing quietly away on one of his merchant ships. If she was traveling illegally, he was able to grease enough palms to make sure that no one noticed or reported her. Because communication was more difficult at that time, he was able to use his influence and money to restore her reputation. She was still only 18 years old, and if rumors about her pirate career did reach anyone's ears they would likely disregard the stories as being wholly unlikely for a girl so young.

Not long after they returned to Charleston, Anne met a local man named Joseph Burleigh, who was somewhat older than her and was well known to her father. As they got to know each other, she may have told him about her checkered past or she may have simply portrayed herself as the young, pretty widow of a dead sea captain with whom she had a child. If Burleigh did have any misgivings about their future together, it is likely that Anne's father's fortune soon put those concerns to rest. The two married on December 21, 1721, when Anne was 19 years old.

Having sown her wild oats, Anne apparently settled down into the kind of domestic life she had previously been to restless to accept. According to the records, she and Burleigh lived the rest of their lives as happy, respected members of the Charleston community. She bore and raised 10 more children, living to see most of them grow to adulthood and marry. By the time she died, on April 22, 1782, she had grandchildren and great-grandchildren. She was buried in the Burleigh family plot in the York County Churchyard in York County, Virginia.

Chapter 10: Legacies

As pirates go, Calico Jack, Anne Bonny and Mary Read were not the meanest or kindest, nor were they the strongest or weakest. Calico Jack was not a successful pirate, and he is remembered more for his association with Anne Bonny and Mary Read than anything else. The same could be said for both Anne Bonny and Mary Read as well; their piracy was in no way remarkable aside from the fact that they were women.

While Calico Jack contributed to the stereotypes of pirates through the use of his "Jolly Roger" pirate flag and his colorful attire, the fact that Anne Bonny and Mary Read were women has become a legacy unto itself. Anne Bonny has passed down through history as a strong-willed independent girl who was fearless and wild enough to become just the kind of pirate people think of today when they hear the term. At the same time, her legend and reputation have a strong historical foundation Even by today's standards, to have been born the illegitimate daughter of a lawyer and his mistress is enough to turn heads. While modern political scandals have softened the public's sensibilities to such misdeeds as adultery, to bring a child into the picture is certain to call one's character into question. Likewise, to abandon one family and move half-way around the world to start another is more the thing of romance novels than it is of real life. And yet, that was precisely what Anne's formative years consisted of, along with being dressed like a boy and told to act like one.

Then there was the matter of her own personality. To harm or even threaten another person with a kitchen knife would land today's teenager in therapy at least, but Anne was simply ignored as the spoiled daughter of a wealthy plantation owner. Anne certainly wasn't encouraged to continue her rebellious ways, but she clearly didn't suffer any serious consequences for her actions either. Even Anne's decision to elope and run away is hardly an unusual story; plenty of young women have run away with men who were disliked by their families. And Anne's affinity for men who were rebellious like her also probably drew her to Calico Jack.

The story of a rebellious headstrong teenage girl who runs away with a bad boy is one that has played out in other settings and environments across history, but what makes Anne unique is that she happened to become a well-known pirate. While she was never a particularly effective one, and may not even have been interested in being one but for her feelings toward Calico Jack, the fact that Anne Bonny became known by name during the Golden Age of Piracy and the mystery surrounding her fate have helped maintain her legend. Throw in her association with another famous woman pirate like Mary Read, and the story becomes even better. To the degree that any pirate can be respected or celebrated, the stories and legends surrounding Anne Bonny have made her a unique and unlikely symbol for any independent woman striving to live outside of conventional society's norms and/or simply be as good as the boys at their own game.

The life, death, and legacy of Mary Read also captured the imaginations of everyone from historians to novelists, and feminists to masochists. There are a number of reasons why her story has been so fascinating in the past, and is likely to continue to be for years to come, beginning with the mystery of her childhood. It is well known that she was raised by her mother as if she had been a male child, and because she was illegitimate, many have speculated that her father may have himself been a sailor and maybe even a pirate. Was Mary born with a thirst for the sea and adventure, or was it simply a necessary evil for Mary's mother to support the family after her husband died?

Perhaps the most remarkable aspect of Mary's life was her sexual identity. At times, she embraced the male lifestyle that had been created for her and was perpetuated by her. During her brief marriage, she also seemed happy enough to live as a woman, only to return to the man's world and life at sea. In a similar vein, legend has it that Mary Read was openly bisexual, equally comfortable in romantic relationships with men and women, but it's also possible that stories of her romance with Anne Bonny were exaggerated just to add to the mystique of the female pirates. Likewise, there is no record of Anne Bonny being attracted to other women, while it is well documented that she had a long term affair with Calico Jack. And even if the three were at one time all lovers, Mary soon fell in love with the nameless seaman for whom she risked her life. Regardless of what is true and false, and what is documented history and unsubstantiated legend, Mary Read has captured the public imagination as being one of the only two well-documented female pirates in the so-called "Golden Age of Piracy."

In an age and society where the freedom of women was greatly restricted, Mary Read and Anne Bonny lived a life at sea as full members of a pirate crew. As subsequent generations increasingly romanticize piracy and the likes of Calico Jack, Anne Bonny and Mary Read, their stature continues to grow even further.

Calico Jack, Anne Bonny and Mary Read's Entries in A General History of the Pyrates

THIS John Rackam, as has been mentioned in the last Chapter, was Quarter-Master to Vane's Company, till they were divided, and Vane turned out for refusing to board and fight the French Man of War; then Rackam was voted Captain of that Division that remained in the Brigantine. The 24th of November 1718, was the first Day of his Command, and his first Cruize was among the Caribbee Islands, where he took and plunder'd several Vessels.

We have already taken Notice, that when Captain Woodes Rogers went to the Island of Providence, with the King's Pardon to such as should surrender, this Brigantine, which Rackam now commanded, made its Escape, thro' another Passage, bidding Defiance to Mercy.

To Windward of Jamaica, a Madera Man fell into the Pyrates Way, which they detained two or three Days, till they had made their Market out of her, and then gave her back to the Master, and permitted one Hosea Tisdell, a Tavern-Keeper at Jamaica, who had been pick'd up in one of their Prizes, to depart in her, she being then bound for that Island.

After this Cruize, they went into a small Island and cleaned, and spent their Christmas ashore, drinking and carousing as long as they had any Liquor left, and then went to Sea again for more, where they succeeded but too well, though they took no extraordinary Prize, for above two Months, except a Ship laden with Thieves from Newgate, bound for the Plantations, which, in a few Days, was retaken with all her Cargo, by an English Man of War.

Rackam stood off towards the Island of Burmudas, and took a Ship bound to England from Carolina, and a small Pink from New-England, and brought them to the Bahama Islands, where with the Pitch, Tar, and Stores, they clean'd again, and refitted their own Vessel; but staying too long in that Neighbourhood, Captain Rogers, who was Governor of Providence, hearing of these

Ships being taken, sent out a Sloop well mann'd and arm'd, which retook both the Prizes, and in the mean while the Pyrate had the good Fortune to escape.

From hence they sailed to the Back of Cuba, where Rackam kept a little kind of a Family, at which Place, they staid a considerable Time, living ashore with their Dalilahs, till their Money and Provision were expended, and then they concluded it Time to look out: They repaired to their Vessel, and was making ready to put Sea, when a Guarda del Costa came in with a small English Sloop, which she had taken as an Interloper on the Coast. The Spanish Guardship attack'd the Pyrate, but Rackam being close in behind a little Island, she could do but little Execution where she lay, therefore the Spaniard warps into the Channel that Evening, in order to make sure of her the next Morning. Rackam finding his Case desperate, and hardly any Possibility of escaping, resolved to attempt the following Enterprize: The Spanish Prize lying for better Security close into the Land, between the little Island and the Main; Rackam takes his Crew into the Boat, with their Pistols and Cutlashes, rounds the little Island, and falls aboard their Prize silently in the dead of the Night, without being discovered, telling the Spaniards that were aboard of her, that if they spoke a Word, or made the least Noise, they were dead Men, and so became Master of her; when this was done, he slipt her Cable, and drove out to Sea: The Spanish Man of War, was so intent upon their expected Prize, that they minded nothing else, and assoon as Day broke, made a furious Fire upon the empty Sloop, but it was not long before they were rightly apprized of the Matter, and cursed themselves for Fools, to be bit out of a good rich Prize, as she prov'd to be, and to have nothing but an old crazy Hull in the room of her.

Rackam and his Crew had no Occasion to be displeased at the Exchange, that enabled them to continue some Time longer in a Way of Life that suited their depraved Tempers: In August 1720, we find him at Sea again, scouring the Harbours and Inlets of the North and West Parts of Jamaica, where he took several small Craft, which proved no great Booty to the Rovers, but they had but few Men, and therefore they were obliged to run at low Game, till they could encrease their Company.

In the Beginning of September, they took seven or eight Fishing-Boats in Harbour Island, stole their Nets and other Tackle, and then went off the French Part of Hispaniola, and landed, and took Cattle away, with two or three French Men they found near the Water-Side, hunting of wild Hogs in the Evening: The French Men came on Board, whether by Consent or Compulsion, I can't say. They afterwards plundered two Sloops, and returned to Jamaica, on the North Coast of which Island, near Porto Maria Bay, they took a Scooner, Thomas Spenlow Master; it was then the 19th of October. The next Day, Rackam seeing a Sloop in Dry Harbour Bay, he stood in and fired a Gun; the Men all run ashore, and he took the Sloop and Lading, but when those ashore found them to be Pyrates, they hailed the Sloop, and let them know they were all willing to come aboard of them.

Rackam's coasting the Island in this Manner, proved fatal to him, for Intelligence came to the

Governor, of his Expedition, by a Canoa which he had surprized ashore, in Ocho Bay; upon which a Sloop was immediately fitted out, and sent round the Island in quest of him, commanded by Captain Barnet, with a good Number of Hands. Rackam rounding the Island, and drawing near the Westermost Point, called Point Negril, saw a small Pettiauger, which at sight of the Sloop, run ashore and landed her Men; when one of them hailed her, Answer was made, They were English Men, and desired the Pettiauger's Men to come on Board, and drink a Bowl of Punch, which they were prevailed upon to do; accordingly the Company came all aboard of the Pyrate, consisting of nine Persons, in an ill Hour; they were armed with Muskets and Cutlashes, but, what was their real Design by so doing, I shall not take upon me to say; but they had no sooner laid down their Arms, and taken up their Pipes, but Barnet's Sloop, which was in Pursuit of Rackam's, came in Sight.

The Pyrates finding she stood directly towards her, fear'd the Event, and weighed their Anchor, which they but lately let go, and stood off: Captain Barnet gave them Chace, and having the Advantage of little Breezes of Wind, which blew off the Land, came up with her, and, after a very small Dispute, took her, and brought her into Port Royal, in Jamaica.

In about a Fortnight after the Prisoners were brought ashore, viz. November 16, 1720, a Court of Admiralty was held at St. Jago de la Vega, before which the following Persons were convicted, and Sentence of Death passed upon them, by the President, Sir Nicholas Laws, viz. John Rackam Captain, George Fetherston Master, Richard Corner Quarter-Master, John Davis, John Howell, Patrick Carty, Thomas Earl, James Dobbin and Noah Harwood. The five first were executed the next Day at Gallows Point, at the Town of Port Royal, and the rest, the Day after, at Kingston; Rackam, Feverston and Corner, were afterwards taken down and hang'd up in Chains, one at Plumb Point, one at Bush Key, and the other at Gun Key.

But what was very surprizing, was, the Conviction of the nine Men that came aboard the Sloop the same Day she was taken. They were try'd at an Adjournment of the Court, on the 24th of January, waiting all that Time, it is supposed, for Evidence, to prove the pyratical Intention of going aboard the said Sloop; for it seems there was no Act of Pyracy committed by them, after their coming on Board, as appeared by the Witnesses against them, who were two French Men taken by Rackam, off from the Island of Hispaniola, and deposed in the following Manner.

'That the Prisoners at the Bar, viz. John Eaton, Edward Warner, Thomas Baker, Thomas Quick, John Cole, Benjamin Palmer, Walter Rouse, John Hanson, and John Howard, came aboard the Pyrate's Sloop at Negril Point, Rackam sending his Canoe ashore for that Purpose: That they brought Guns and Cutlashes on Board with them: That when Captain Barnet chased them, some were drinking, and others walking the Deck: That there was a great Gun and a small Arm fired by the Pyrate Sloop, at Captain Barnet's Sloop, when he chased her; and that when Captain Barnet's Sloop fired at Rackam's Sloop, the Prisoners at the Bar went down under Deck. That during the Time Captain Barnet chased them, some of the Prisoners at the Bar (but which of them he could not tell) helped to row the Sloop, in order to escape from Barnet: That they all seemed to be consorted together.

This was the Substance of all that was evidenced against them, the Prisoners answered in their Defence,

'That they had no Witnesses: That they had bought a Pettiauger in order to go a Turtleing; and being at Negril Point, and just got ashore, they saw a Sloop with a white Pendant coming towards them, upon which they took their Arms, and hid themselves in the Bushes: That one of them hail'd the Sloop, who answer'd, They were English Men, and desired them to come aboard and drink a Bowl of Punch; which they at first refused, but afterwards with much perswasion, they went on Board, in the Sloop's Canoe, and left their own Pettiauger at Anchor: That they had been but a short Time on Board, when Captain Barnet's Sloop heaved in Sight: That Rackam ordered them to help to weigh the Sloop's Anchor immediately, which they all refused: That Rackam used violent Means to oblige them; and that when Captain Barnet came up with them, they all readily and willingly submitted.

When the Prisoners were taken from the Bar, and the Persons present being withdrawn, the Court considered the Prisoners Cases, and the Majority of the Commissioners being of Opinion, that they were all Guilty of the Pyracy and Felony they were charged with, which was, the going over with a pyratical and felonious Intent to John Rackam, &c. then notorious Pyrates, and by them known to be so, they all received Sentence of Death; which every Body must allow proved somewhat unlucky to the poor Fellows.

On the 17th of February, John Eaton, Thomas Quick and Thomas Baker, were executed at Gallows Point, at Port Royal, and the next Day John Cole, John Howard and Benjamin Palmer, were executed at Kingston; whether the other three were executed afterwards, or not, I never heard.

Two other Pyrates were try'd that belonged to Rackam's Crew, and being convicted, were brought up, and asked if either of them had any Thing to say why Sentence of Death should not pass upon them, in like Manner as had been done to all the rest; and both of them pleaded their Bellies, being quick with Child, and pray'd that Execution might be stay'd, whereupon the Court passed Sentence, as in Cases of Pyracy, but ordered them back, till a proper Jury should be appointed to enquire into the Matter.

NOW we are to begin a History full of surprizing Turns and Adventures; I mean, that of Mary Read and Anne Bonny, alias Bonn, which were the true Names of these two Pyrates; the odd Incidents of their rambling Lives are such, that some may be tempted to think the whole Story no better than a Novel or Romance; but since it is supported by many thousand Witnesses, I mean the People of Jamaica, who were present at their Tryals, and heard the Story of their Lives, upon the first discovery of their Sex; the Truth of it can be no more contested, than that there were such Men in the World, as Roberts and Black-beard, who were Pyrates.

Mary Read was born in England, her Mother was married young, to a Man who used the Sea, who going a Voyage soon after their Marriage, left her with Child, which Child proved to be a Boy. As to the Husband, whether he was cast away, or died in the Voyage, Mary Read could not tell; but however, he never returned more; nevertheless, the Mother, who was young and airy, met with an Accident, which has often happened to Women who are young, and do not take a great deal of Care; which was, she soon proved with Child again, without a Husband to Father it, but how, or by whom, none but her self could tell, for she carried a pretty good Reputation among her Neighbours. Finding her Burthen grow, in order to conceal her Shame, she takes a formal Leave of her Husband's Relations, giving out, that she went to live with some Friends of her own, in the Country: Accordingly she went away, and carried with her her young Son, at this Time, not a Year old: Soon after her Departure her Son died, but Providence in Return, was pleased to give her a Girl in his Room, of which she was safely delivered, in her Retreat, and this was our Mary Read.

Here the Mother liv'd three or four Years, till what Money she had was almost gone; then she thought of returning to London, and considering that her Husband's Mother was in some Circumstances, she did not doubt but to prevail upon her, to provide for the Child, if she could but pass it upon her for the same, but the changing a Girl into a Boy, seem'd a difficult Piece of Work, and how to deceive an experienced old Woman, in such a Point, was altogether as impossible; however, she ventured to dress it up as a Boy, brought it to Town, and presented it to her Mother in Law, as her Husband's Son; the old Woman would have taken it, to have bred it up, but the Mother pretended it would break her Heart, to part with it; so it was agreed betwixt them, that the Child should live with the Mother, and the supposed Grandmother should allow a Crown a Week for it's Maintainance.

Thus the Mother gained her Point, she bred up her Daughter as a Boy, and when she grew up to some Sense, she thought proper to let her into the Secret of her Birth, to induce her to conceal her Sex. It happen'd that the Grandmother died, by which Means the Subsistance that came from that Quarter, ceased, and they were more and more reduced in their Circumstances; wherefore she was obliged to put her Daughter out, to wait on a French Lady, as a Foot-boy, being now thirteen Years of Age: Here she did not live long, for growing bold and strong, and having also a roving Mind, she entered her self on Board a Man of War, where she served some Time, then quitted it, went over into Flanders, and carried Arms in a Regiment of Foot, as a Cadet; and tho' upon all Actions, she behaved herself with a great deal of Bravery, yet she could not get a Commission, they being generally bought and sold; therefore she quitted the Service, and took on in a Regiment of Horse; she behaved so well in several Engagements, that she got the Esteem of all her Officers; but her Comrade who was a Fleming, happening to be a handsome young Fellow, she falls in Love with him, and from that Time, grew a little more negligent in her Duty, so that, it seems, Mars and Venus could not be served at the same Time; her Arms and

Accoutrements which were always kept in the best Order, were quite neglected: 'tis true, when her Comrade was ordered out upon a Party, she used to go without being commanded, and frequently run herself into Danger, where she had no Business, only to be near him; the rest of the Troopers little suspecting the secret Cause which moved her to this Behaviour, fancied her to be mad, and her Comrade himself could not account for this strange Alteration in her, but Love is ingenious, and as they lay in the same Tent, and were constantly together, she found a Way of letting him discover her Sex, without appearing that it was done with Design.

He was much surprized at what he found out, and not a little pleased, taking it for granted, that he should have a Mistress solely to himself, which is an unusual Thing in a Camp, since there is scarce one of those Campaign Ladies, that is ever true to a Troop or Company; so that he thought of nothing but gratifying his Passions with very little Ceremony; but he found himself strangely mistaken, for she proved very reserved and modest, and resisted all his Temptations, and at the same Time was so obliging and insinuating in her Carriage, that she quite changed his Purpose, so far from thinking of making her his Mistress, he now courted her for a Wife.

This was the utmost Wish of her Heart, in short, they exchanged Promises, and when the Campaign was over, and the Regiment marched into Winter Quarters, they bought Woman's Apparel for her, with such Money as they could make up betwixt them, and were publickly married.

The Story of two Troopers marrying each other, made a great Noise, so that several Officers were drawn by Curiosity to assist at the Ceremony, and they agreed among themselves that every one of them should make a small Present to the Bride, towards House-keeping, in Consideration of her having been their fellow Soldier. Thus being set up, they seemed to have a Desire of quitting the Service, and settling in the World; the Adventure of their Love and Marriage had gained them so much Favour, that they easily obtained their Discharge, and they immediately set up an Eating House or Ordinary, which was the Sign of the Three Horse-Shoes, near the Castle of Breda, where they soon run into a good Trade, a great many Officers eating with them constantly.

But this Happiness lasted not long, for the Husband soon died, and the Peace of Reswick being concluded, there was no Resort of Officers to Breda, as usual; so that the Widow having little or no Trade, was forced to give up House-keeping, and her Substance being by Degrees quite spent, she again assumes her Man's Apparel, and going into Holland, there takes on in a Regiment of Foot, quarter'd in one of the Frontier Towns: Here she did not remain long, there was no likelihood of Preferment in Time of Peace, therefore she took a Resolution of seeking her Fortune another Way; and withdrawing from the Regiment, ships herself on Board of a Vessel bound for the West-Indies.

It happen'd this Ship was taken by English Pyrates, and Mary Read was the only English Person on Board, they kept her amongst them, and having plundered the Ship, let it go again;

after following this Trade for some Time, the King's Proclamation came out, and was publish'd in all Parts of the West-Indies, for pardoning such Pyrates, who should voluntarily surrender themselves by a certain Day therein mentioned. The Crew of Mary Read took the Benefit of this Proclamation, and having surrender'd, liv'd quietly on Shore; but Money beginning to grow short, and hearing that Captain Woods Rogers, Governor of the Island of Providence, was fitting out some Privateers to cruise against the Spaniards, she with several others embark'd for that Island, in order to go upon the privateering Account, being resolved to make her Fortune one way or other.

These Privateers were no sooner sail'd out, but the Crews of some of them, who had been pardoned, rose against their Commanders, and turned themselves to their old Trade: In this Number was Mary Read. It is true, she often declared, that the Life of a Pyrate was what she always abhor'd, and went into it only upon Compulsion, both this Time, and before, intending to quit it, whenever a fair Opportunity should offer it self; yet some of the Evidence against her, upon her Tryal, who were forced Men, and had sailed with her, deposed upon Oath, that in Times of Action, no Person amongst them were more resolute, or ready to Board or undertake any Thing that was hazardous, as she and Anne Bonny; and particularly at the Time they were attack'd and taken, when they came to close Quarters, none kept the Deck except Mary Read and Anne Bonny, and one more; upon which, she, Mary Read, called to those under Deck, to come up and fight like Men, and finding they did not stir, fired her Arms down the Hold amongst them, killing one, and wounding others.

This was part of the Evidence against her, which she denied; which, whether true or no, thus much is certain, that she did not want Bravery, nor indeed was she less remarkable for her Modesty, according to her Notions of Virtue: Her Sex was not so much as suspected by any Person on Board, till Anne Bonny, who was not altogether so reserved in point of Chastity, took a particular liking to her; in short, Anne Bonny took her for a handsome young Fellow, and for some Reasons best known to herself, first discovered her Sex to Mary Read; Mary Read knowing what she would be at, and being very sensible of her own Incapacity that Way, was forced to come to a right Understanding with her, and so to the great Disappointment of Anne Bonny, she let her know she was a Woman also; but this Intimacy so disturb'd Captain Rackam, who was the Lover and Gallant of Anne Bonny, that he grew furiously jealous, so that he told Anne Bonny, he would cut her new Lover's Throat, therefore, to quiet him, she let him into the Secret also.

Captain Rackam, (as he was enjoined,) kept the Thing a Secret from all the Ship's Company, yet, notwithstanding all her Cunning and Reserve, Love found her out in this Disguise, and hinder'd her from forgetting her Sex. In their Cruize they took a great Number of Ships belonging to Jamaica, and other Parts of the West-Indies, bound to and from England; and when ever they meet any good Artist, or other Person that might be of any great Use to their Company, if he was not willing to enter, it was their Custom to keep him by Force. Among these was a young Fellow of a most engageing Behaviour, or, at least, he was so in the Eyes of Mary Read, who became so smitten with his Person and Address, that she could neither rest, Night or Day; but as there is nothing more ingenious than Love, it was no hard Matter for her, who had before been practiced in these Wiles, to find a Way to let him discover her Sex: She first insinuated her self into his liking, by talking against the Life of a Pyrate, which he was altogether averse to, so they became Mess-Mates and strict Companions: When she found he had a Friendship for her, as a Man, she suffered the Discovery to be made, by carelesly shewing her Breasts, which were very White.

The young Fellow, who was made of Flesh and Blood, had his Curiosity and Desire so rais'd by this Sight, that he never ceased importuning her, till she confessed what she was. Now begins the Scene of Love; as he had a Liking and Esteem for her, under her supposed Character, it was now turn'd into Fondness and Desire; her Passion was no less violent than his, and perhaps she express'd it, by one of the most generous Actions that ever Love inspired. It happened this young Fellow had a Quarrel with one of the Pyrates, and their Ship then lying at an Anchor, near one of the Islands, they had appointed to go ashore and fight, according to the Custom of the Pyrates: Mary Read, was to the last Degree uneasy and anxious, for the Fate of her Lover; she would not have had him refuse the Challenge, because, she could not bear the Thoughts of his being branded with Cowardise; on the other Side, she dreaded the Event, and apprehended the Fellow might be too hard for him: When Love once enters into the Breast of one who has any Sparks of Generosity, it stirs the Heart up to the most noble Actions; in this Dilemma, she shew'd, that she fear'd more for his Life than she did for her own; for she took a Resolution of quarreling with this Fellow her self, and having challenged him ashore, she appointed the Time two Hours sooner than that when he was to meet her Lover, where she fought him at Sword and Pistol, and killed him upon the Spot.

It is true, she had fought before, when she had been insulted by some of those Fellows, but now it was altogether in her Lover's Cause, she stood as it were betwixt him and Death, as if she could not live without him. If he had no regard for her before, this Action would have bound him to her for ever; but there was no Occasion for Ties or Obligations, his Inclination towards her was sufficient; in fine, they applied their Troth to each other, which Mary Read said, she look'd upon to be as good a Marriage, in Conscience, as if it had been done by a Minister in Church; and to this was owing her great Belly, which she pleaded to save her Life.

She declared she had never committed Adultery or Fornication with any Man, she commended the Justice of the Court, before which she was tried, for distinguishing the Nature of their Crimes; her Husband, as she call'd him, with several others, being acquitted; and being ask'd, who he was? she would not tell, but, said he was an honest Man, and had no Inclination to such Practices, and that they had both resolved to leave the Pyrates the first Opportunity, and apply themselves to some honest Livelyhood.

It is no doubt, but many had Compassion for her, yet the Court could not avoid finding her Guilty; for among other Things, one of the Evidences against her, deposed, that being taken by Rackam, and detain'd some Time on Board, he fell accidentally into Discourse with Mary Read, whom he taking for a young Man, ask'd her, what Pleasure she could have in being concerned in such Enterprizes, where her Life was continually in Danger, by Fire or Sword; and not only so, but she must be sure of dying an ignominious Death, if she should be taken alive?—She answer'd, that as to hanging, she thought it no great Hardship, for, were it not for that, every cowardly Fellow would turn Pyrate, and so infest the Seas, that Men of Courage must starve:—That if it was put to the Choice of the Pyrates, they would not have the punishment less than Death, the Fear of which, kept some dastardly Rogues honest; that many of those who are now cheating the Widows and Orphans, and oppressing their poor Neighbours, who have no Money to obtain Justice, would then rob at Sea, and the Ocean would be crowded with Rogues, like the Land, and no Merchant would venture out; so that the Trade, in a little Time, would not be worth following.

Being found quick with Child, as has been observed, her Execution was respited, and it is possible she would have found Favour, but she was seiz'd with a violent Fever, soon after her Tryal, of which she died in Prison."

The LIFE of ANNE BONNY,

AS we have been more particular in the Lives of these two Women, than those of other Pyrates, it is incumbent on us, as a faithful Historian, to begin with their Birth. Anne Bonny was born at a Town near Cork, in the Kingdom of Ireland, her Father an Attorney at Law, but Anne was not one of his legitimate Issue, which seems to cross an old Proverb, which says, that Bastards have the best Luck. Her Father was a Married Man, and his Wife having been brought to Bed, contracted an Illness in her lying in, and in order to recover her Health, she was advised to remove for Change of Air; the Place she chose, was a few Miles distance from her Dwelling, where her Husband's Mother liv'd. Here she sojourn'd some Time, her Husband staying at Home, to follow his Affairs. The Servant-Maid, whom she left to look after the House, and attend the Family, being a handsome young Woman, was courted by a young Man of the same Town, who was a Tanner; this Tanner used to take his Opportunities, when the Family was out of the Way, of coming to pursue his Courtship; and being with the Maid one Day as she was employ'd in the Houshold Business, not having the Fear of God before his Eyes, he takes his Opportunity, when her Back was turned, of whipping three Silver Spoons into his Pocket. The Maid soon miss'd the Spoons, and knowing that no Body had been in the Room, but herself and the young Man, since she saw them last, she charged him with taking them; he very stifly denied it, upon which she grew outragious, and threatned to go to a Constable, in order to carry him before a Justice of Peace: These Menaces frighten'd him out of his Wits, well knowing he could not stand Search; wherefore he endeavoured to pacify her, by desiring her to examine the Drawers and other Places, and perhaps she might find them; in this Time he slips into another

Room, where the Maid usually lay, and puts the Spoons betwixt the Sheets, and then makes his Escape by a back Door, concluding she must find them, when she went to Bed, and so next Day he might pretend he did it only to frighten her, and the Thing might be laugh'd off for a Jest.

As soon as she miss'd him, she gave over her Search, concluding he had carried them off, and went directly to the Constable, in order to have him apprehended: The young Man was informed, that a Constable had been in Search of him, but he regarded it but little, not doubting but all would be well next Day. Three or four Days passed, and still he was told, the Constable was upon the Hunt for him, this made him lye concealed, he could not comprehend the Meaning of it, he imagined no less, than that the Maid had a Mind to convert the Spoons to her own Use, and put the Robbery upon him.

It happened, at this Time, that the Mistress being perfectly recovered of her late Indisposition, was return'd Home, in Company with her Mother-in-Law; the first News she heard, was of the Loss of the Spoons, with the Manner how; the Maid telling her, at the same Time, that the young Man was run away. The young Fellow had Intelligence of the Mistress's Arrival, and considering with himself, that he could never appear again in his Business, unless this Matter was got over, and she being a good natured Woman, he took a Resolution of going directly to her, and of telling her the whole Story, only with this Difference, that he did it for a Jest.

The Mistress could scarce believe it, however, she went directly to the Maid's Room, and turning down the Bed Cloaths, there, to her great Surprize, found the three Spoons; upon this she desired the young Man to go Home and mind his Business, for he should have no Trouble about it.

The Mistress could not imagine the Meaning of this, she never had found the Maid guilty of any pilfering, and therefore it could not enter her Head, that she designed to steal the Spoons her self; upon the whole, she concluded the Maid had not been in her Bed, from the Time the Spoons were miss'd, she grew immediately jealous upon it, and suspected, that the Maid supplied her Place with her Husband, during her Absence, and this was the Reason why the Spoons were no sooner found.

She call'd to Mind several Actions of Kindness, her Husband had shewed the Maid, Things that pass'd unheeded by, when they happened, but now she had got that Tormentor, Jealousy, in her Head, amounted to Proofs of their Intimacy; another Circumstance which strengthen'd the whole, was, that tho' her Husband knew she was to come Home that Day, and had had no Communication with her in four Months, which was before her last Lying in, yet he took an Opportunity of going out of Town that Morning, upon some slight Pretence: —All these Things put together, confirm'd her in her Jealousy.

As Women seldom forgive Injuries of this Kind, she thought of discharging her Revenge upon the Maid: In order to this, she leaves the Spoons where she found them, and orders the Maid to put clean Sheets upon the Bed, telling her, she intended to lye there herself that Night, because her Mother in Law was to lye in her Bed, and that she (the Maid) must lye in another Part of the House; the Maid in making the Bed, was surprized with the Sight of the Spoons, but there were very good Reasons, why it was not proper for her to tell where she found them, therefore she takes them up, puts them in her Trunk, intending to leave them in some Place, where they might be found by chance.

The Mistress, that every Thing might look to be done without Design, lies that Night in the Maid's Bed, little dreaming of what an Adventure it would produce: After she had been a Bed some Time, thinking on what had pass'd, for Jealousy kept her awake, she heard some Body enter the Room; at first she apprehended it to be Thieves, and was so fright'ned, she had not Courage enough to call out; but when she heard these Words, Mary, are you awake? She knew it to be her Husband's Voice; then her Fright was over, yet she made no Answer, least he should find her out, if she spoke, therefore she resolved to counterfeit Sleep, and take what followed.

The Husband came to Bed, and that Night play'd the vigorous Lover; but one Thing spoil'd the Diversion on the Wife's Side, which was, the Reflection that it was not design'd for her; however she was very passive, and bore it like a Christian. Early before Day, she stole out of Bed, leaving him asleep, and went to her Mother in Law, telling her what had passed, not forgetting how he had used her, as taking her for the Maid; the Husband also stole out, not thinking it convenient to be catch'd in that Room; in the mean Time, the Revenge of the Mistress was strongly against the Maid, and without considering, that to her she ow'd the Diversion of the Night before, and that one good Turn should deserve another; she sent for a Constable, and charged her with stealing the Spoons: The Maid's Trunk was broke open, and the Spoons found, upon which she was carried before a Justice of Peace, and by him committed to Goal.

The Husband loiter'd about till twelve a Clock at Noon, then comes Home, pretended he was just come to Town; as soon as he heard what had passed, in Relation to the Maid, he fell into a great Passion with his Wife; this set the Thing into a greater Flame, the Mother takes the Wife's Part against her own Son, insomuch that the Quarrel increasing, the Mother and Wife took Horse immediately, and went back to the Mother's House, and the Husband and Wife never bedded together after.

The Maid lay a long Time in the Prison, it being near half a Year to the Assizes; but before it happened, it was discovered she was with Child; when she was arraign'd at the Bar, she was discharged for want of Evidence; the Wife's Conscience touch'd her, and as she did not believe the Maid Guilty of any Theft, except that of Love, she did not appear against her; soon after her Acquittal, she was delivered of a Girl.

But what alarm'd the Husband most, was, that it was discovered the Wife was with Child also, he taking it for granted, he had had no Intimacy with her, since her last lying in, grew jealous of her, in his Turn, and made this a Handle to justify himself, for his Usage of her, pretending now he had suspected her long, but that here was Proof; she was delivered of Twins, a Boy and a Girl.

The Mother fell ill, sent to her Son to reconcile him to his Wife, but he would not hearken to it; therefore she made a Will, leaving all she had in the Hands of certain Trustees, for the Use of the Wife and two Children lately born, and died a few Days after.

This was an ugly Turn upon him, his greatest Dependence being upon his Mother; however, his Wife was kinder to him than he deserved, for she made him a yearly Allowance out of what was left, tho' they continued to live separate: It lasted near five Years; at this Time having a great Affection for the Girl he had by his Maid, he had a Mind to take it Home, to live with him; but as all the Town knew it to be a Girl, the better to disguise the Matter from them, as well as from his Wife, he had it put into Breeches, as a Boy, pretending it was a Relation's Child he was to breed up to be his Clerk.

The Wife heard he had a little Boy at Home he was very fond of, but as she did not know any Relation of his that had such a Child, she employ'd a Friend to enquire further into it; this Person by talking with the Child, found it to be a Girl, discovered that the Servant-Maid was its Mother, and that the Husband still kept up his Correspondence with her.

Upon this Intelligence, the Wife being unwilling that her Children's Money should go towards the Maintenance of Bastards, stopped the Allowance: The Husband enraged, in a kind of Revenge, takes the Maid home, and lives with her publickly, to the great Scandal of his Neighbours; but he soon found the bad Effect of it, for by Degrees lost his Practice, so that he saw plainly he could not live there, therefore he thought of removing, and turning what Effects he had into ready Money; he goes to Cork, and there with his Maid and Daughter embarques for Carolina.

At first he followed the Practice of the Law in that Province, but afterwards fell into Merchandize, which proved more successful to him, for he gained by it sufficient to purchase a considerable Plantation: His Maid, who passed for his Wife, happened to dye, after which his Daughter, our Anne Bonny, now grown up, kept his House.

She was of a fierce and couragious Temper, wherefore, when she lay under Condemnation, several Stories were reported of her, much to her Disadvantage, as that she had kill'd an English Servant-Maid once in her Passion with a Case-Knife, while she look'd after her Father's House; but upon further Enquiry, I found this Story to be groundless: It was certain she was so robust, that once, when a young Fellow would have lain with her, against her Will, she beat him so, that he lay ill of it a considerable Time.

While she lived with her Father, she was look'd upon as one that would be a good Fortune, wherefore it was thought her Father expected a good Match for her; but she spoilt all, for without his Consent, she marries a young Fellow, who belonged to the Sea, and was not worth a Groat;

which provoked her Father to such a Degree, that he turned her out of Doors, upon which the young Fellow, who married her, finding himself disappointed in his Expectation, shipped himself and Wife, for the Island of Providence, expecting Employment there.

Here she became acquainted with Rackam the Pyrate, who making Courtship to her, soon found Means of withdrawing her Affections from her Husband, so that she consented to elope from him, and go to Sea with Rackam in Men's Cloaths: She was as good as her Word, and after she had been at Sea some Time, she proved with Child, and beginning to grow big, Rackam landed her on the Island of Cuba; and recommending her there to some Friends of his, they took Care of her, till she was brought to Bed: When she was up and well again, he sent for her to bear him Company.

The King's Proclamation being out, for pardoning of Pyrates, he took the Benefit of it, and surrendered; afterwards being sent upon the privateering Account, he returned to his old Trade, as has been already hinted in the Story of Mary Read. In all these Expeditions, Anne Bonny bore him Company, and when any Business was to be done in their Way, no Body was more forward or couragious than she, and particularly when they were taken; she and Mary Read, with one more, were all the Persons that durst keep the Deck, as has been before hinted.

Her Father was known to a great many Gentlemen, Planters of Jamaica, who had dealt with him, and among whom he had a good Reputation; and some of them, who had been in Carolina, remember'd to have seen her in his House; wherefore they were inclined to shew her Favour, but the Action of leaving her Husband was an ugly Circumstance against her. The Day that Rackam was executed, by special Favour, he was admitted to see her; but all the Comfort she gave him, was, that she was sorry to see him there, but if he had fought like a Man, he need not have been hang'd like a Dog.

She was continued in Prison, to the Time of her lying in, and afterwards reprieved from Time to Time; but what is become of her since, we cannot tell; only this we know, that she was not executed."

Bibliography

Brown, Douglas. (1962). *Anne Bonny, Pirate Queen: The True Saga of A Fabulous Female Buccaneer.* Monarch Books.

Creighton, Margartet and Lisa Norling. (1996). *Iron Men, Wooden Women: Gender and Seafaring in the Atlantic World, 1700-1920.* Gender Relations in the American Experience.

Defoe, Daniel and Manuel Schonhorn (1999). The General History of Pirates. New York: Dover Publications.

Eastman, Tamara J. and Constance Bond. (2000). The Pirate Trial of Anne Bonny and Mary

Read. Fern Canyon Press.

Johnson, Captain Charles, ed. Hayward Arthur L., "A history of the robberies and murders of the most notorious pirates from their first rise and settlement in the island of Providence to the present year", George Routledge & Sons, Ltd. London.

Johnson, Pamela. (2009). Heart of a Pirate: A Novel of Anne Bonny. Stone Harbour Press.

Kaserman, James and Sarah. Florida Pirates: From the Southern Gulf Coast to the Keys and Beyond (The History Press) (Nov 16, 2011).

Meltzer, Milton; Waldman, Bruce (2001). *Piracy & Plunder: A Murderous Business*. New York: Dutton Children's Books.

Nash D. A. (2012) The Profligate: The Legend of Anne Bonny by D.A. NASH (Jun 5, 2012)

Nelson, James L. (2004). *The Only Life That Mattered: The Short and Merry Lives of Anne Bonny, Mary Read, and Calico Jack Rackam*. McBooks Press.

Riley, Sandra. (2003). *Sisters of the Sea: Anne Bonny & Mary Read, Pirates of the Caribbean*. Riley Hall.

Sharp, Anne Wallace (2002). *Daring Pirate Women*. Minneapolis: Lerner Publications.

Utley, Stephen. (2012) *Anne Bonny*. CreateSpace Independent Publishing Platform.

Vantana, Karen and Becky Weaver (2010). *Anne Bonny: The Legend of a Female Pirate*. CreateSpace Independent Publishing Platform.

Weintraub, Aileen. (2005). *Anne Bonny and Mary Read: Fearsome Female Pirates of the Eighteenth Century*. Tony Stead Nonfiction Independent Reading Collections.

Williams, Jeffrey S. (2007). *Pirate Spirit: The Adventures of Anne Bonney*. iUniverse Star.

Made in the USA
Coppell, TX
18 October 2022